My Favorite Miracles

"I thought it good to declare the signs and wonders that the Most High God has worked for me. How great are His signs and how mighty His wonders."
- Daniel 4:2-3

Silver A. Fisher
www.SilverFisher.com

Introduction

~~~

I am almost 60 years old now. What have I learned? Life
is miraculous, God is real, and He absolutely loves us. Each
chapter in this book contains a unique miracle that God
performed in My life in the order in which they occurred.
All credit for the miracles in my life belong to God Almighty
and my Lord and Savior Jesus Christ.

Generally, when people say the word "miracle," a lot of
different ideas and opinions usually surface. In simplest
form, miracles are unexplainable events. Often times,
people will refer to miracles like blessings or rewards.
This often means that the modern reference to a miracle,
is usually an unexplainable event that provides us with
some sort of benefit or gain. However, when we think about
miracles, we really need to consider two things. First, that
the work is God's work, done by His hands, according to
His purposes. These works are, as such, often well-beyond
our comprehension. We aren't always going to understand
God's work or why He's doing it. The Bible states the
following about this:

*Have you not known? Have you not heard? The everlasting
God, the LORD, The Creator of the ends of the earth, neither
faints nor is weary. His understanding is unsearchable.
– Isaiah 40:28*

Oh, the depth of the riches both of the wisdom and knowledge of God! How unsearchable are His judgments and His ways past finding out!
– Romans 11:33

Keep these simple truths in mind when reading my life stories. Notice that sometimes God produces difficulties and victories – both of which were miraculous. Remember that God is the author of miracles. He will show favor and trials to whomever He wants, whenever He wants. When it comes to miracles, it is important to worship God himself, not the effects of God's works and miracles.

Contents

Silver Is My Name

~~~

"But rise and stand upon your feet, for I have appeared to you for this purpose, to appoint you as a minister and a witness both of the things in which you have seen and of the things which I wil yet reveal to you..."
- Acts 26:16

My Dad owned a nightclub. Mom stayed home raising the sons, four in total, one more on the way. One night, Mom, very pregnant by this point, walked into Dad's nightclub intending to bring her husband some food. What she found was that he wasn't exactly there at the counter, working, serving beer as he usually was. In reality, he was busy having an adulterous affair with one of his barmaids in the back seat of the family car. Needless to say, when she found him, she was devastated. Anguish, is what she felt. It sucked the life out of her. She swore to leave him and abort the child in her womb.

The image kept coming back to her, back to what felt like her soul. She regretted the abortion. The emotions deepened and the pain of catching my father in the affair, combined with the guilt of ending what could have been a beautiful life drove my mother to the brink. Her life became too painful and she considered suicide on a daily basis. My mother decided there were only two ways out of her emotional pain: the first was to take her own life and leave her 4 boys motherless; and the second was to call out to God. She knew she couldn't leave her boys without a mother and so she put her hope and healing in the hands of the Lord. She wept and cried out to God Almighty and yet could not forgive herself. On her knees she prayed to God, promising Him that if He would grant her another son, she would continuously pray for the baby and - just as Hanna in the Bible did - she would give the baby back to the Lord. Hanna said:

"I prayed for this child, and the LORD has granted me what I asked of Him. So now I give him to the LORD. For his whole life he will be given over to the LORD."
- 1 Samuel 1:27-28 (NIV)

My mother continued to call out to God and He answered her prayers. God began to restore her marriage with my father, removing her anguish and healing her heart.

Eventually, God gave my mother a gift. Another pregnancy. She prayed throughout the pregnancy promising to dedicate her "miracle baby" to God. Nine months passed and she gave birth to a healthy 7-pound baby boy. She felt happy for her gift and wanted to name her son something special. Silver, she decided, would be his name.

Hello, my name is Silver Fisher and I am that "miracle baby." When I was 30 years old my mother told me this story. She had never told anyone this before. Here is a direct quote from my mom:

"Silver when you were born I cried tears of joy!"

Unknown to my mother at the time, the Bible uses silver (the precious metal) as a symbol of forgiveness and redemption. God forgave my mother for the abortion and filled her with love to replace the emptiness. In Godlike fashion He put my name in her heart along with the willingness to receive its message.

When my mom told me this story it reaffirmed my purpose:

To seek God with all my heart as she did despite many obstacles.

I came to realize that God has a love and purpose for all of us, one that we can only find by seeking Him. God has a great life-plan for you specifically. No one else on this planet can deliver the unique message that you were created to deliver, nor receive the unique miracles you were created to receive.

The Bible says:

"'For I know the thoughts that I think toward you,' says the LORD, 'Thoughts of peace and not of evil, to give you a future and a hope. Then you will call upon Me and go and pray to

Me, and I will listen to you. And you will seek Me and find
[Me], when you search for Me with all your heart."
– Jeremiah 29:11-13

Have you ever wondered what your purpose in life is?
We all have, I think. My job here is to tell you that you can
find the answers written in the Bible. Your purpose is to
seek and find God. When you seek Him and find Him, your
purpose will be revealed to you. You will find your meaning
through God's unique path for your life. God will guide you
to the people you need to hear from and also the people
who need to hear from you. He will prepare you for these
encounters and give you the words to say. Every day is an
opportunity for you to hear God's message and deliver it to
someone else.

The book of Esther in the Bible is a great example of this.
Esther was placed into a lofty position in the king's palace.
After years of living in royalty, Esther was called upon by
God to risk her life and use her influence to speak to the
king and save the Jews. She was afraid and God sent her this
message:

"For if you remain completely silent at this time, relief and
deliverance will arise for the Jews from another place, but you
and your father's house will perish. Yet who knows whether
you have come to the kingdom for [such] a time as this?"
–Esther 4:14

In God's perfect timing, Esther was prepared in the
perfect place and was called upon by God to fulfill her
purpose in life. She obeyed God and helped save the Jews
from extinction. You can live your life surrounded by the
comfort of God's blessings, as Esther did in the palace, but
your true purpose, your God-given purpose, may be well
outside of that comfort zone. Whether God gives you one
task or blesses you with many, your purpose is necessary.
Whatever your calling, you were most certainly born for

God's purpose. God knows every cell in your body. You are as unique as the plans that God has for you. Seek God and you will not only find your life purpose but you will find God.

Being Punished

~~~

"But you [are] a chosen generation, a royal priesthood, a holy nation, His own special people, that you may proclaim the praises of Him who called you out of darkness into His marvelous light..."
- 1 Peter 2:9

It was Saturday morning. We were on the front lawn, my brothers and I, wearing army fatigues and green barrettes, balanced on our behinds, with feet off the ground, heads suspended, pounding our stomachs like ape chests. We were crying. My Dad with dark red hair and a build like a boxer stood over us hollering like a drill sergeant. Bone, Four-eyes, Jackass, I don't remember all of them, but these were our names. Watching one of my brothers get kicked, getting dragged off to the bathroom where he'd be beaten, all for putting his feet down - that was worse than getting punished myself. We were not allowed to be children. We were soldiers, punished for our weakness.

At the age of four one of my weaknesses was fear of the dark. My father found this particularly unacceptable. To rid me of this fear, my father would lock me inside a small closet for hours at a time. In this closet, I would pray. God and I became very close in those early days as He guided me out of the darkness and into His spiritual light.

Every morning my father woke us up at 4:00 AM. Hollering, slapping, hitting, cursing and name calling; these were our alarms. My four older brothers and I would line up in the bathroom for our daily freezing-cold shower. One-by-one (I was always first), he'd grab us by the neck and throw us into the icy water, the others shaking and standing at attention. He'd grab the current brother, pull him out of the shower and shove the next one into the water. We would all shiver, we would all cry, but no one would leave until everyone was done.

In my mind I compare this morning ritual to POW's being beaten and water-boarded. There'd be more hollering, my dad would run us out of the bathroom, we'd be standing at attention within minutes: military surplus army boots (too small), green berets with airborne patches (sewn by our mother), and backpacks filled with weights. We'd do two hours in the park before school: pushups, sit-ups, rope climbing, bar-dips, sprints, fighting tactics. My father would kick us, curse at us, pit brother against brother. By the time we finished, we were drenched and breathing hard.

Next we'd sit in the car, windows up, heater on high, for 20minutes to "sweat it out" as he called it. No water. Another long cold shower awaited us before we could eat and go to school.

Our father would regularly shave our heads white. We'd walk into the classroom in what seemed like unison, everyone in the classroom would point and laugh at us (this was the 60's, long hair was in). At recess, at lunch, they'd continue laughing. We were careful not to shower or expose our bodies at school, for fear of anyone seeing our black and purple striped welts across our backs and butts, from the belt. If anyone from the school called the cops, we'd just be in for more punishment of being hung upside down naked, whipped with a leather belt, a cord, and a fist.

I wanted to be tough for my father, to show him that he could be proud of me. I didn't want to cry because he despised weakness and showing him my tears only caused more punishment. I'd always hold it in for as long as I could, taking the beatings without crying. Be tough. Come on, you can do it. Be tough I would say to myself, eventually giving in to the torture and crying out in horror. I'd beg him to stop as he hit me with the belt repeatedly. "Get on the table and write 500 pages," He'd say, out of breath. "I will keep my closet clean from now on because I know it is the right thing to do."

My father said later that he wanted to make sure we were tougher than the other kids, to make sure we banded together. Possibly with the right psychology he would have accomplished his goal, but what he did instead was create a destructive childhood that tore our family apart. He was on a mission to make us perfect and we were simply not, we were just five boys trying to survive our childhood.

One night, I was having a particularly bad night at home, my beatings were no longer just from my father, but now included beatings from my four older brothers as they became angrier by the year. I went out to the park by my house one night to pray and be alone with God. This night the sky was overcast and full of clouds. I couldn't see any stars, only the dark cloudy sky. I remember kneeling in the wet soaking grass. I remember looking hard and praying:

"Lord I need to see You tonight. I need to see the stars. Please God. I need to see that You are with Me."

As I knelt there at the center of the park surrounded by darkness, I heard God's still small voice speak to my heart.

God said, "Silver, do you see the stars?"

I said, "No Lord, I do not see the stars. I only see clouds."

He replied, "Do you believe that they are there?"

I responded, "Yes Lord, I believe that the stars are there."

Then the Lord said to me, "So am I, and even though you cannot see Me and sometimes you do not feel Me, I am always there; loving you and embracing you Silver."

I felt goosebumps all over me. I was certain it was God speaking.

The Bible says in Romans 8:28:

"And we know that God causes all things to work together for good to those who love God, to those who are the called according to His purpose." - NASB

What an amazing promise that God makes in this scripture! During our tough times, He will bring forth blessings, perhaps here on earth; but most certainly in Heaven. I want you to take special note of the word "ALL" in this scripture.

The Bible does not say that God causes some things to work together for good. It doesn't say that God causes most things to work together for good. God causes ALL things to work together for good and the only prerequisites are that we love God and are called according to His purpose. This means that every event in our life, the seemingly good and the bad, will collectively produce good.

There are great examples in the Bible which demonstrate that God causes all things to work together for good: the testimonies of Joseph, Job, and Daniel, just to name a few. These were men who loved God and were called according to His purpose just like you and me.

Joseph was sold into slavery by his jealous brothers, was wrongly accused, and thrown in jail to await his death. God saved him from his punishment, and promoted him to prominent leadership in Egypt. God did this to use Joseph according to His good purposes, to save an entire nation from a famine. God did not take Joseph from his time of slavery and imprisonment, even though he was innocent. He let Joseph deal with those difficulties by learning to pray and rely on God.

Job was a man of God and he was tested by Satan and had his house, his kids, his livestock, and his health stripped from him. God did not spare Job from the pain and agony of the test where he learned humility and a deeper trust in God through prayer. God did, however, preserve Job's faith, spiritual integrity, and life and went on to abundantly restore his health, wealth, and even gave him a new family.

Daniel was a man of God and he was thrown into a lion's den. God saved Daniel from being eaten by the lions and eventually promoted him to second in charge in the Babylonian Empire, but God did not save Daniel from spending the night in the lion's den and learning to rely on Him in fearful situations.

The Bible says in John 16:33:

"I have told you these things, so that in me you may have peace. In this world you will have trouble. But take heart! I have overcome the world." - NIV

When I was consistently thrown into that dark closet at a very young age, I learned to pray in my darkness and through my trials. I learned to pray all night long because that was how I received peace. When I got older, this was perhaps one of the greatest gifts I ever received. I learned to connect with my Heavenly Father in my darkness, trials, and tough times.

Another memorable night, I was there again, kneeling in that park, my beautiful stars covered by darkness and storm clouds. I called out to God with tears in my eyes, saying to myself that He is here, He is with me. In the middle of my prayer, I lifted my hands to worship Him, and as I opened my eyes and uncurled my fingers, I watched as God tore those clouds apart to show me the most spectacular stars I had ever seen. It was as if God had reached down and moved those clouds with His own hands just for me, a small clay figure in the middle of the park, to view them; my hands raised to heaven smiling and worshipping Him as best as I knew how.

Yes, God Himself, the Creator of all the universe loves you in a special and unique way. He is always with you and is so very present and powerful.

Poisoning Dad

~~~

"But in all [things] we commend ourselves as ministers of God: in much patience, in tribulations, in needs, in distresses, in stripes, in imprisonments, in tumults, in labors, in sleeplessness, in fastings; by purity, by knowledge, by longsuffering, by kindness, by the Holy Spirit, by sincere love, by the word of truth, by the power of God, by the armor of righteousness on the right hand and on the left, by honor and dishonor, by evil report and good report; as deceivers, and [yet] true..."
- II Corinthians 6:4-8

Arsenic, a deadly poison - one that would end my father's life and all of our suffering. In 1967 my mother had just finished mixing an entire bottle of arsenic into my father's mashed potatoes, when she heard a knock at the door. My mom had grown weary of my father's horrendous verbal and physical abuse towards us, so she decided to put an end to it once and for all - but that would have to wait a second.

At the door were two elderly ladies speaking to the local neighbors about God. They began to talk to my mom about God's forgiveness and His will for her life. As they spoke, tears filled my mother's eyes and after several minutes she finally broke down and confessed: she was about to poison my father with arsenic. The two elderly ladies folded their hands, bowed their heads and solemnly prayed with my mom in the doorway. They assured her that God had a purpose for the pain we all experience, and that He would help our family through this dark time. After they left, my mom poured the poisoned potatoes down the sink. The elderly ladies saved my father's life and my mom from a life laden with horrendous guilt and imprisonment.

That prayer changed my mom forever. She became a passionate, devoted Christian, and at the age of five, I followed in her footsteps. We were constantly sneaking off to church where we would hear stories about courageous Bible characters and their horrific trials. My mom and I could relate so closely because we were going through similar things ourselves. Some Sundays I would sneak out and walk to church by myself while my mom distracted my father.

My mom and I had faith in God, which brought more beatings and humiliation from my father. If I wanted to attend church with her, my father made me wear a dress and lipstick. Many times, my mom and I were afraid, but God was so present and so real to us that we were willing to risk the pain and humiliation to be closer to Him. God gave us strength and motivation to continue the good fight of faith. We enjoyed listening to such stories like Shadrach, Meshach & Abednego braving the fiery furnace; Daniel confronting the lion's den; and David defeating Goliath. Sometimes I felt like my father was bigger than Goliath and more ferocious than the lions. Frequently after church my mom and I would drive slowly past the house to see if it was safe to go inside, hoping that my father wasn't home and that the beating would be delayed, if only for a short time. We were checking for huge piles of our belongings - clothing, shoes, towels, food, dishes, silverware, blankets, plants, books and bedding from the house, that my father would pile on our front lawn as retaliation for our sneaking out to go to church. As my mom and I drove around the block, several times looking at the pile in the front yard, we would pray and cry out to God for His protection from my father's' wrath, for strength, and help.

One time in particular when my mom and I came home to a huge pile of stuff on the front lawn, instead of my dad hitting us, he said, "Just clean up the mess outside; I'm not going to hit you." WOW that was amazing! God had answered our long-awaited prayers, with a small but significant miracle. For the first time God had softened my dad's heart. We praised God with joy in our hearts for this day as we put our things back into the house where they belonged. Those were the times we knew God had answered our prayers and that He was moving to protect us.

Those were both amazing and tough times. In those days, I would pray for hours in secret places: In that dark, once-scary closet, in the dirty garage among old car parts and spider webs, and of course, at the park every night under the stars. Wherever I was, God met me there and I found meaning and great peace in His presence.

My dad did not stop his punishment altogether but he was

becoming more lenient towards my mom and I attending church and studying the Bible. We knew God was loving us by softening my dad's heart. We continued to grow in our faith and trust in God. As our love for God grew, my mom and I became so willing to take punishment for what we believed. God was with us in many of our trials. The miracles are too numerous to name.

Eventually my father began, somehow, letting us welcome believers into our home to discuss the Bible. God is good. God is gracious. God is kind, and God is patient.

As the years passed, my father grew old and became very ill. As his body began to fail him, he would lay on his sickbed and ask my mom to sing Christian songs to comfort him. In 2002, before my father died of cirrhosis of the liver, he asked for our forgiveness and asked Christ into his heart. That is one of God's greatest miracles! My father died a saved man and is now in Heaven with Christ.

God will not save you from every trial - believe me, my mom and I are living proof of that. The Bible says God is faithful and will never leave you or forsake you. God is always there with us, as He was with my mom and I in our trail, and with my dad at the end of his life.

The Bible says in I Corinthians 15:58:

"Therefore, my beloved brethren, be steadfast, immovable, always abounding in the work of the Lord, knowing that your labor is not in vain in the Lord."

Born Again!

~~~

Jesus answered him and said, "Truly, truly I say to you, unless one is born again he cannot see the kingdom of God"
- John 3:3 (ESV)

Jesus answered, "I am the way the truth and the life. No one comes to the Father except through me."
- John 14:6 (NIV)

There I was on the phone with a friend of mine named Terri Davis. I listened as she explained what it meant to be "born again." I had heard the term before, but had never taken any steps to actually accomplish being "born again." Terri pointed out a very revealing Bible scripture that basically said, if you have Christ, you have eternal life in heaven. If you do not have Christ, you do not have eternal life in heaven.

She was referring to 1 John 5:11-13. It was really quite simple to me. I needed no other explanation. I had felt God work throughout my childhood giving me strength and comfort when my dad and brothers would beat me time and time again. The act of simply saying a sincere prayer and asking Jesus in my heart was small compared to all God had done for me throughout my childhood.

When I said the simple prayer of asking God's forgiveness for all of my past, present, and future sins, and asked Jesus Christ to come into my heart, the sky didn't open. The Red Sea didn't split in two, and I didn't hear any deep voices calling me from Heaven. However, I did feel different, like a miraculous cleansing had taken place in my soul. I somehow received a revelation that all of my childhood and teenage sins had been forgiven, washed away. Just like Terri explained would happen, it happened. I was born again and I felt it.

Drowning

~~~

But as they sailed He fell asleep. And a windstorm came down on the lake, and they were filling [with water], and were in jeopardy. And they came to Him and awoke Him, saying, "Master, Master, we are perishing!" Then He arose and rebuked the wind and the raging of the water. And they ceased, and there was a calm.
- Luke 8:23-24

At the age of four, I was thrown into the deep end of a swimming pool. My body and head were completely immersed underwater. The only thing above the waterline were my tiny fingers trying frantically to get someone's attention. I was drowning. I couldn't swim. I couldn't scream for help. I could no longer hold my breath. Ready to give up and allow the pool water to enter my lungs, I heard a loud splash behind me and felt someone grab me and lift me up out of the depths. My brother Danny had saved my life. This near-death experience left a lingering fear of deep water in the back of my mind.

Years later when I was a teenager, I was invited by some friends to go snorkeling. Having never snorkeled before, I eagerly snuck out of the house and jumped in my friends' car. We drove to some small jagged cliffs off of San Pedro. The sun was shining and the ocean water was warm and perfect. My friends handed me some fins for my feet, a snorkel, and a mask. I was scared but eager to learn. My feet stepping off the rocky shore into the clear blue ocean, my face lowering into the water, and I was amazed at how clearly I could see with the mask on. More importantly, I was excited to see how easily I could breathe through the snorkel!

Below me in the water, I spotted some colorful fish, which I decided to follow for a while. Following them as they maneuvered through the water, I lost track of time and space. Suddenly, I was swimming through several hundred strands of tall seaweed. I tried to swim out from among them, but I couldn't. My fins and hands became tangled in the seaweed. I began to panic.

The memory of nearly drowning as a child entered my mind. The more I struggled, the murkier the water became, salt water filling my mask and snorkel. I continued to panic, as my vision became darkened and blurred, more water entered the snorkel, preventing me from breathing. With each attempted breath, I swallowed more water. My panic became uncontrollable as I tried to untangle my fins from the strands. Once again I was in desperate trouble with no one near to save me.

Unable to hold my breath any longer, I cried out with all my heart to God. "Oh God, please help me, I don't want to die today." God's voice came so clearly to me at that moment:

"Thrust to the bottom of the ocean and spring up as hard as you can to the top of the water and break the grip of the seaweed."

With all of my strength and power, gulping water, I pushed myself to the bottom of the ocean and I thrust myself up from the seaweed bed, out of the water and frantically ripped off my snorkel and mask and inhaled a deep breath of fresh air. Simultaneously, I realized that I was standing in waist-high water. Yes, waist high water! My friends sat 10 yards from me on the rocks, laughing and joking about my unusual snorkeling technique. They had no idea the fear that had gripped me having nearly panicked myself to death in a few feet of water.

I was crying, shocked, embarrassed, and happy all at the same time. Ironically, my drowning memory almost killed me. God's voice was so loud that day and I was in awe of His presence when I needed Him most. A profound lesson continues to unfold itself, make itself clear, as I return to this memory again and again; God calls upon all of us to spring up out of our past entanglements and to become free in Christ Jesus.

For me, I would find out that day that my calling is to be a PRAYER WARRIOR, one who calls out to God on behalf of others. It's fitting that the seed of that calling saved me that day. There is no way that some wet plants and waist high water could have kept me down and drowned me. What kept me down was the memory of a past circumstance, the imagination of the size and grip of the seaweed. As ridiculous as the situation was in hindsight, what saved me was calling out to God, who helped me see how small the problem really was compared to Him.

Our "problems" in life can seem insurmountable and much bigger than our ability to handle them. We often look into our past to find circumstances similar to ones we are going through. We can become deathly entangled in our fear and imagination. Suddenly we are looking death in the eye and forgetting that God is with us in every circumstance in this life and promises to uphold us with His righteous right hand.

The Bible says in Isaiah 41:10:

"Do not fear, for I am with you; do not anxiously look about you, for I am your God. I will strengthen you, surely I will help you, surely I will uphold you with My righteous right hand."

What a glorious promise God makes to us personally! He promised to lift us up with His righteous hand, enabling us to spring up in the midst of seemingly insurmountable circumstances, saying to the devil, "You are a liar and I am alive to serve God almighty and I will go home to be with the Lord when He has ordained me to, and not a moment sooner."

God wants us to stand on His promises knowing that He will help us through all of our troubles, no matter the size. I learned a valuable lesson that day that has stuck with me throughout the years, one that I can call upon when I feel that life is drowning me. We often panic in life over things that are shallow in God's eyes. If we pray and call out to God, He will strengthen us to spring from trials into a fresh new moment of comfort. Listen for His voice. He may not solve your problems, but He will help you rise above them.

"Therefore we do not lose heart. Even though our outward man is perishing, yet the inward [man] is being renewed day by day. For our light affliction, which is but for a moment, is working for us a far more exceeding [and] eternal weight of glory, while we do not look at the things which are seen, but at the things which are not seen. For the things which are seen [are] temporary, but the things which are not seen [are] eternal.."
- II Corinthians 4:16-18

Saving A College Student

~~~

"Go therefore and make disciples of all the nations, baptizing them in the name of the Father and of the Son and of the Holy Spirit, teaching them to observe all things that I have commanded you; and lo, I am with you always, [even] to the end of the age." Amen.
- Matthew 28:19-20

One day I was at the library looking for books. I found some good ones and sat at a table already occupied by several people immersed in their own reading, taking notice of a well-dressed young gentleman with dark hair sitting across from me. He appeared to be in his early 20's. As I sat down, we made eye contact and said hello to one another. Within a few moments, I was prompted by God to ask if he was a Christian. I looked at him from across the table and quietly asked, "Do you know Jesus and is He your personal Lord and Savior?"

"Oh My God! I don't believe this!" The guy looked at me, speaking very loudly.

"I'm sorry!" I whispered, shushing him with my finger, looking around. "Sorry, I will just read my book."

"No, you don't understand. This is crazy," he replied.

"Wha -- What do you mean?" I stammered.

"My sister is a Christian and she told me I was going to have an encounter with God today. My sister told you to ask me, didn't she?" He asked.

"No. I don't know your sister."

"You've got to be joking. You don't know my sister? Then why did you ask me about Jesus?"

The entire table was now listening to our conversation.

"Please hold your voice down, I promise I do not know your sister nor did she put me up to doing this. I'm a Christian and that is why I asked you that question." I said, trying to keep my voice soft.

We left the library together and talked outside about what

it means to receive Jesus. His name was Gilbert and he was an agnostic. After his experience this day, this moment in the library, this miracle, Gilbert was quite convinced that there must be a God. Gilbert attended church with me that Sunday and gave his life to Christ. He became a fired-up Christian. We eventually lost touch but I do believe God caused Gilbert's sister to tell him that he would have a Godly encounter that day and God caused me to speak to Gilbert. God called Gilbert out of the crowd to be spoken to that day. God had a calling for Gilbert's life and I was the vessel He chose to make it apparent to him.

The Bible says...

"Eye has not seen, nor ear heard, nor has it entered into the heart of man that which God has prepared for those that love Him."
- I Corinthians 2:9

I am in awe of God. He is always performing miracles and demonstrating His love. Often, the whisper of God's still small voice prompting us to talk to someone gets ignored. If you step out in faith and speak to others about God, you will receive His tremendous blessings, as I did while speaking with Gilbert. That's what's in store for those who obey - a life filled with wonderment, amazement and blessings.

The more you obey the Holy Spirit, the clearer His voice becomes; and the less you obey His voice, the fainter His voice becomes.

Trying To Sin

~~~

"Come now, and let us reason together,"
Says the LORD, "Though your sins are
like scarlet, they shall be as white as
snow; though they are red like crimson,
they shall be as wool."
- Isaiah 1:18

It was a particularly hot day in Southern California. On this day, young, vigorous, foolish and unmarried, I was tempted to sin. I was trying to be a man of God, reaching deep within myself to remain pure for the woman that God might put in my path someday. Temptation was everywhere and I found it increasingly difficult to remain pure and faithful. I would pray and fast for days sometimes, but impure thoughts would get the better of me. One day I started looking through the troves of personal ads for adult services.

One ad caught my attention. It was posted by a woman, who performed "adult entertainment" in her Hollywood apartment. I called this woman and asked if I could come to her apartment and she graciously invited me to join her. She asked that I call her from a phone booth located on a particular corner in Hollywood when I arrived.

I got in my car and drove that long hour to Hollywood. I can recall parking my car at the corner where the woman told me to call her from. There were at least six phone booths lined up next to each other. I picked up the first phone to call her and the phone was dead, unusable and the second phone had the same issue. As I continued down the line of phone booths, each one proved to be broken. There was a homeless person sitting next to the line of phones. He flagged me down.

"I'll tell you why all the phone booths are broken for a dollar."

I paid him. He said that a man had come by with a sledge hammer earlier that morning and broke all of the phone booths in the area. I thanked him and started searching everywhere for a pay phone that worked. I started feeling like I desperately needed to call this woman. I began to walk in the blazing hot sun with my pocket full of quarters. Each phone booth I put in my quarter, dialed her number and none of them worked. As I walked block after block trying all the phones were broken.

Soon, I found myself six blocks away from my car, running low on quarters. I came to the understanding, as I panted and walked, that this encounter was not God's plan for me. He was keeping me out of trouble. God was not going to allow me to find a working phone booth. Frustrated, I cried out to Him and said, "Lord I'm just bored and hot. Please let me find a phone booth that works and I will call my brother Danny and ask if he wants to go to the movies instead of calling this woman."

Immediately after the prayer, a strange thing happened. The very next phone booth I tried had worked. I stared into the sky in amazement. I put my quarter in the slot, dialed the phone number, and listened to one beep after another as I pushed the numbers. The phone rang and my brother Danny answered. I proceeded to ask him if he would go to the movies with me. Danny's response was music to my ears, "I would love to go to the movies with you, Silver." God had faithfully answered my prayers!

As I took those first few steps away from the phone booth, I began to rejoice, but as I did a small thought crept in my mind. I could now use that phone booth to call the woman providing the "adult entertainment". The thought kept growing, taking root deeper and deeper into my thoughts as the temptation became stronger. Suddenly, I turned back toward that phone booth, taking one step after another and said in a low toned voice, "I'm sorry God, I guess I fooled you. I'm going to call that woman."

I walked those five steps back to that exact same phone booth, picked up the receiver and the phone was dead. I put in more quarters, pressed buttons again and again, hit the phone with the palm of my hand several times, hung up and started again, but the phone was utterly and completely dead. I may as well have had a piece of wood in my hand. I couldn't make any call, let alone that sinful call I wanted to make to that woman. I could not get the phone to work no matter how hard I tried.

I got so frustrated that I began to weep and was scared, happy, and completely astonished all at the same time. I thought I had fooled God, but in fact God had fooled me. He knows your heart and your thoughts, friends. I felt God's love at that moment but was scared about the reality of His ability to interact with me at such a detailed level.

I felt defeated and distraught, yet amazed at the reality of God. Head down with tear-filled eyes I began the long walk back toward my car. It was extremely hot, and sweat beaded on my forehead. I stepped into an anonymous commercial building to cool off in the air-conditioned space for a while. I stood there staring at my reflection in the window crying and thinking what a terrible sinner I am. Just then, I felt a hand on my leg. I turned around to see and old woman in a wheelchair looking up at me. In fact, there was a whole room full of elderly women, probably pushing 90-years old, all in wheelchairs and walkers, staring at me. I think they were just as surprised by my appearance as I was by theirs. They had gathered behind me as I gazed out that window, cooling off and pondering my sin. They began to approach me, several of them placing their hands on my legs, asking if I was there to visit someone.

"No, I'm not visiting anyone. I'm just a rotten sinner trying to get out of the hot sun," I told them.

"What are you doing here, honey?" They asked again.

"I am here in Hollywood sinning and I need prayer for God to bring me a wife," I answered, flustered.

Like The Red Sea at Moses' command, the wheelchairs and walkers parted and a large elderly dark-skinned woman in a wheelchair rolled through the crowd toward me. In a very stern voice she ordered me to get on my knees.

"Huh?" I responded, perplexed.

"Get on your knees!" She commanded.

That time I obeyed her. I humbly and tearfully folded my body to the floor, got on my knees, closed my eyes, and folded my hands in prayer. I felt her warm hands on my head as she asked in a strong voice, "Boy, what is it that you want from God?"

I replied, "I want a wife so I can stop being sinful."

I could hear her amazingly strong voice as she began to sing the most powerful prayer-filled song I had ever heard.

"He's a good boy Lord! Bring him a wife Lord! He l-o-v-e-s you Lord. Bring him a wife Lord."

Over and over she repeated this song as the other elderly ladies quietly clapped and hummed in the background. There I was knelt down in front of this powerful prayer warrior singing to God as I was on my knees sobbing. Over and over she repeated the song.

"He's a good boy Lord! Bring him a wife Lord! He l-o-v-e-s you Lord. Bring him a wife Lord."

After 10 minutes they finished singing and praying for me. I felt God's love all over me. I felt a sense of renewal, overwhelmed with the feeling that God had forgiven me and that He understood everything. I was broken but forgiven on my knees. God was present in that old commercial building.

I was so moved by love coming from my new elderly

friends. I was willing to do anything for them. With my renewed spirit I asked, "What can I do for all of you?" Someone said, "Well, the food here is terrible." I looked her straight in the eye and nodded, then, without skipping a beat, I ran out the door and headed straight for a hot dog cart situated across the street. I bought some hot dogs then ran to a donut shop next door and bought a bunch of donuts. When I went back into the brick commercial building I handed out the hot dogs and donuts. These elderly people and I began to party. We sang Christian songs together, we rejoiced in the blessings that God had given to all of us that day. Everyone was happy. I led them in the song:

"Put your hand in the hand of the man that stills the water."

We sang to the Lord in praise for all He had done for us that day.

A nurse walked in on our party and said, "Who the hell gave the patients hot dogs and donuts?" They all pointed to me but held on dearly to their food. They would not give them up to the nurse. The nurse actually tried to take the food from them and they wrenched and turned to keep her from being able to snag their food away. The nurse asked me to leave and I did, but I rejoiced all the way back to my car singing, "I am a good boy Lord. Bring me a wife Lord. Bless me Lord." God's love was all over me.

For months, I went back several times to visit with those elderly ladies. One night I visited the building and I looked through the front glass door and saw Emma, one of the eldest ladies, sitting on an old chair in the lobby area all by herself. The facility was closed so I put my hand against the glass door and she placed her palm against mine as we smiled at each other through the locked glass doors. I reached into my pocket and pulled out a $20 bill and slid it through the small opening between the doors. She took the twenty and held it to her heart and as she began to sob. I came back a week later to visit Emma and the nurse told me that she had died of loneliness. I was blessed to know that as misguided as my initial intentions were, I brought some joy into the life of some older believers. I can still recall the sweet face of Emma, and the rest of those saints that God put in my path, with their beautiful voices singing, partying and enjoying those hot dogs and donuts.

My Last $20

~~~

*Let them shout for joy and be glad,
who favor my righteous cause; and let
them say continually, "Let the LORD
be magnified, Who has pleasure in the
prosperity of His servant."*
– Psalms 35:27

Mobile home in Cypress, California, first month's mortgage paid, I stared into my empty refrigerator, mostly just cold white walls staring back, with the exception of a couple tortillas and a bottle of ranch dressing. I had a twenty-dollar bill that needed to get me to the end of next week. The neighborhood church was having service that morning, so I decided to go. I sat third row from the back, raising my hands in praise as the band played. I wore a fake gold watch on my left wrist, self-consciously. That morning's sermon was about "giving". The pastor encouraged his congregation to honor the Lord with their wealth. I sat there listening, wondering how I could share my wealth when I had none, fake gold watch notwithstanding, hands in pockets, folding my only twenty. The sermon ended, the band started up again and the collection basket came around, and I (reluctantly would be an understatement) dropped my crumpled $20 bill, along with its promise of food, into the depths of the offering basket. My pockets were now officially empty. As I finished my church pleasantries I walked out, nervous but smiling. Back at my new place, the fridge was still empty.

"Good morning!" I waved to the guard and walked through to the data center doors as I had every day for a year. I heard the mainframes humming, computer operators typing commands into consoles, and my stomach loudly protesting that $20 offering of mine. I spent the day running batch jobs, mounting tapes, and banging out commands, silently thinking that perhaps giving my food money wasn't such a good idea. I walked out of work dressed in a suit with empty pockets, looking for my car in the parking lot. Payday was on Friday, so this was going to be a long week, I thought, trying to put together some ways to make ranch and tortillas palatable. Suddenly, a dark-haired man in catering truck pulled up next to me, interrupting my reverie.

"You want something to eat?" He asked.

"No thank you, I don't have any money," I replied.

"Don't worry about it man, I'm trying to build my business in this area."

Suit and tie on, I was thinking, why would he offer me free food? He knows I'm not poor. With a big smile on his face, he hopped out of the driver's seat and opened the side of the truck. As the door swung up, I saw a woman there smiling, ready to cook for me.

"Order anything you'd like," the man said. I ordered a cheeseburger with fries, grabbed a dessert, a carton of milk, some pumpkin seeds, a cinnamon roll and some Fritos. As I stood there with my arms full, I asked, "Are you sure this is okay with you? I don't have any money."

With a smile he replied, "Absolutely!"

I was greatly astonished. I knew without a doubt that this was a miracle from God. He was showing me how much He loved me and a return on my $20 offering. Perhaps another blessing for being faithful to Him? I noticed a small chain around the catering truck drivers' neck, at the bottom of this chain was a small cross of Jesus.

I said to him, "WOW! Can I tell you about the miracle that just happened here?"

"I have to get going now," he responded, closing the side door, climbing into his truck and speeding off. I ate my food and as I drove home, I was in awe of the love of God for me.

It didn't end there. As I pulled up to my mobile home, I opened my car door and got out, I saw a plate of enchiladas on my doorstep with a note that said:

"Welcome to the Neighborhood!"

I was amazed. God had really come through for me again. As I stepped into the house my phone started ringing. I answered the phone and someone from the church I attended invited me to a BBQ at their house. I ate BBQ ribs that night and they gave me most of the leftovers. I ate the entire week by the miraculous gifts that God had provided to me. It was absolutely amazing. God is certainly in the business of miracles!

"But this [I say]: He who sows sparingly will also reap sparingly, and he who sows bountifully will also reap bountifully. [So let] each one [give] as he purposes in his heart, not grudgingly or of necessity; for God loves a cheerful giver."
– 2 Corinthians 9:6-7

When I gave that $20, I did not give a lot by society's standards, but I gave all that I had and that was enough to enact God's miraculous love and power into my life. God understands the worth of our sacrifices. He understands the value of the things we give, whether that be time, or money. He knows how to reward us for giving.

There is an invisible law in effect called, "The Law of the Harvest." It's a farming principal that states when we plant wheat, we wait, and then the harvest will grow. I cannot see the law of giving and receiving, and neither can I see the law of the harvest, but I can see the fruits of both flourishing in a life when we give. At this point in my walk with Christ, I no longer care if I receive back. I believe, because I've seen too much to deny the reality that when I give, I receive. Of course, in order for you to see the results of giving, you must first give. Giving is the only subject in which God invites us to test Him.

"Bring all the tithes into the storehouse, that there may be food in My house, and try Me now in this," Says the LORD of hosts, "If I will not open for you the windows of heaven and

pour out for you [such] blessing that [there will] not [be room] enough [to receive it]."
– Malachi 3:10

I don't have the ability to predict or explain how, or why, or when God does perform His miracles. Our giving doesn't always provoke miracles from God; His blessings come in many varieties. But He will often reward us if our motives are righteous.

He loves a cheerful giver He's interested in the intentions behind our gifts.

Do we test God to seek God, or test Him to get something from Him? I have often sat in awe and wonder if God would have provided the catering truck, the enchiladas or the BBQ, had I not given that $20 at church.

Either way, God is REAL! He proves it in many ways. In this instance He proved it through a miracle that proved His faithfulness. He loves us and He does perform miracles, especially, it seems, when we step out in faith and in giving.

Dating Karen

~~~

But the LORD inflicted serious diseases on Pharaoh and his household because of Abram's wife Sarai. So Pharaoh summoned Abram. "What have you done to me?" he said. "Why didn't you tell me she was your wife? Why did you say, 'She is my sister,' so that I took her to be my wife? Now then, here is your wife. Take her and go!" Then Pharaoh gave orders about Abram to his men, and they sent him on his way, with his wife and everything he had.
– Genesis 12:17-20 (NIV)

There was a steel basin of water that I used to keep on the floor of the room adjacent to my bedroom. My alarm clock went next to it along with my Bible, opened to a random page. I'd used the water to wake myself up, splashing it in my face at 3:00 AM every morning before kneeling down for an hour of prayer. This morning was no different: My car was broken down in the driveway and I was walking to work at 4:00 AM in order to arrive by 8:00 AM.

This lasted a month. It turned out that the catalytic converter had melted. Some old man had figured this out with a wire hanger, something that countless mechanics with elaborate machines had missed. Either way, I was driving to work again, waking up at 4:00 instead of 3:00, no basin, walking out of my house carrying cardboard boxes filled with Bibles to pass out at work.

Many of the government guards were brothers and sisters in Christ so they appreciated the gesture and actually started handing out Bibles themselves. I worked for a defense contractor, managing computers for black-ops projects. Non-professional, let alone religious, activities were not allowed. This ban forced the guards and I underground. We'd sneak out and pray in the machine rooms or the mechanical closets and conduct quick Bible studies where no one would see us. Within the month, I began seeing strangers in the break and lunch rooms reading those Bibles. I would be eating lunch with Karen, a woman I was dating at the time, soft-spoken with blue eyes and dark hair. She'd smile at me knowing that God was working in our lives.

One evening after work I was driving home, a 70's Chevy pulled up next to my Porsche at a stoplight. The driver of the blue Chevy waved at me to catch my attention, gesturing, trying to get me to roll down the window. I expected him to ask directions but instead he said:

"By any chance, is your name Silver?"

I told him yes and he said, "Would you mind pulling over for a few minutes?"

This was an odd request, but I thought perhaps he knew me from work; after all, we were only a block away from my office. I agreed and pulled my car into an empty parking lot, with the man following close behind me.

"Are you dating a woman named Karen?"

He started walking faster toward me. With no time to think about his question I remained silent, uncertain how to reply. He started moving faster and then asked me even louder, "Are you dating Karen?"

"Yeah, why?" I responded.

"Because that's my f*%#* wife!"

He started running towards me, cussing and yelling. I stood there in shock for a moment as he pulled his fist back to hit me.

"WAIT, WAIT, WAIT!" I blurted. "I didn't know Karen was married. I haven't even touched her or kissed her." I yelled out, speaking the truth. "I'M A BORN-AGAIN CHRISTIAN!"

His arm came to an abrupt stop inches from my face. He dropped it to his side and began to cry. He reached out to hug me.

"Are you really a Christian?" He asked.

"YES, I am!" I emphasized.

"Please. Please pray for my wife and I," he whimpered.

"We've been separated for months. I miss her. Please pray for us."

My heart broke for Chris as I prayed for a long time with him that night. I promised him I'd break up with his wife and leave her alone. He apologized.

Later that night I called Karen and told her what happened. I broke up with her. The experience had shocked the love out of me, so I felt, simply, like I was doing what needed to be done. Chris reported to me that after several months of counseling that he and Karen got back together and renewed their marriage vows. I am so thankful that I never touched this man's wife. Even though she was a Christian, it was not right for her to start dating me. Had I known she was married/separated I would have declined the invitation to date her.

"[The righteous] cry out, and the LORD hears, and delivers them out of all their troubles. The LORD [is] near to those who have a broken heart, and saves such as have a contrite spirit.
– Psalms 34:17-18

Chris had been praying for his marriage to be restored. I am thankful that I treated Karen with respect as a Christian. I want a blessed life and the only way to accomplish that is to be a strong Christian. When you follow God, He will protect you. God's protection is part of His love for us. Does God protect us from every circumstance? No. If I had not been pure with Karen I believe I would have ended up fighting her husband and losing that fight. When you date, do the honorable things and be the honorable person God created you to be.

The Homeless Lady

~~~

For not from the east, nor from the west,
Nor from the desert [comes] exaltation;
but God is the Judge; He puts down one
and exalts another.
– Psalms 75:6-7 (NASB)

One day I saw an elderly, poor, skinny, homeless woman walking into the grocery store with this small, frail dog. Instead of a dog leash, the poor homeless woman held one end of a long stretched out wire coat hanger with the other end wrapped around her dog's neck.

As I strolled through the store doing my shopping, I saw this woman in various aisles. She stared at the cheapest bread in the bread aisle, then she walked over to the pharmacy and spoke to someone there. She seemed to inspect everything but put very little in her shopping basket. As I stood in line to pay for my groceries, I noticed that the woman was in line right behind me, a loaf of bread and a medicine bottle in her cart. I didn't speak to her. Instead, I quietly asked the check-out clerk working the cash register to allow me to pay for her items as well. The clerk obliged and added them to my bill. I paid without her noticing and then went on my way.

Years went by. One cold evening I was visiting a small community church around Christmas. I took a seat in the back row. The people were singing Christmas carols, laughing and talking. It smelled like apple cider. At the end of the sermon in this warm little church, we all clapped as the pastor concluded by asking if anyone wanted to give a testimony about their favorite miracle that God had done in their lives. One person after another stood and gave their testimony, each with an amazing miracle of their own.

The last testimony was a frail elderly woman, as she stood to her feet she began her testimony by saying,

"A few years ago, I was living on the streets, poor and hungry and couldn't afford any food. In fact, one day I was so broke, I had to choose between buying my prescription medication and a loaf of bread. I was very hungry, yet very sick. The Holy Spirit spoke to me saying, 'Bring both the medicine and the bread to the check-out stand'. It seemed ridiculous to me when I knew I couldn't afford them both, but I obeyed God and took the medicine and the food. Then a wonderful miracle happened. When I reached the checkout person he said to me, 'Ma'am, your items have already been paid for.' I said, 'Boy, I can't understand you. Just tell me how much it is so I can put something back.' The clerk repeated, 'Everything you have has already been paid for ma'am!'"

It was that moment, the lady standing giving her testimony from the front row of the church, turned and pointed at me and said, "That man right there paid for it all! He bought my groceries and my medicine and never said a word to me. He just walked out of the store after paying for everything. That is my favorite miracle God has ever done for me."

The entire church turned towards me, rose to their feet, and gave me a standing ovation for a small act of kindness that I had done years before. Somehow that woman knew that I was the one who had paid for her groceries and her medicine. I was graciously humbled by her story and moved to tears by the once homeless woman and her dog on the wire coat hanger leash.

Miraculously, I had been going through a trial and needed encouragement, and with this moment God delivered a unique message to me that I was loved and appreciated by Him and others. What an amazing God we serve! He knows exactly what we need and when we need it. All things that you do out of the goodness of your heart, every act of faith, every sacrifice is noticed by Him. He is an amazing God, that's for sure.

"And let us not grow weary while doing good, for in due season we shall reap if we do not lose heart. Therefore, as we have opportunity, let us do good to all, especially to those who are of the household of faith."
– Galatians 6:9-10

God is always watching for an opportunity to bless you and to show you His love. Give God a reason to bless you by undertaking the temperament of His own nature. Listen to the leading of the Holy Spirit and be gracious to those who cannot afford to repay you.

In Europe, there is a beautiful statue of Jesus with His arms held out as if to give something to passersby. However, the hands of this statue were blown off during a war. After the war ended, the towns' people wanted to replace the hands of Jesus' statue, but instead of replacing the hands, they decided to mount a plaque in front of the statue that reads:

"I have no hands except yours."

That statue is so beautiful. It represents what Jesus said:

"My little children, let us not love in word or in tongue, but in deed and in truth."
– 1 John 3:18

Saved From Suicide

~~~

"If My people who are called by My name will humble themselves, and pray and seek My face, and turn from their wicked ways, then I will hear from heaven, and will forgive their sin and heal their land."
– II Chronicles 7:14

I'd prefer to write my life story as if it were pure and wholesome, but this chapter and much of what follows is about how God stays with us and guides us even when we are struggling through our sins. Remember the trials I went through as a child, I could easily make excuses for the ways I've behaved later in life. However, I would rather take responsibility for my lack of discipline and self-control. I fought the good fight for years by fasting with just water for several days, praying for an hour straight at 4:00AM, memorizing 100 scriptures and running 10 miles a day to quell my fleshly desires. All of this may sound like trying to earn salvation through works, but my intention was never to earn salvation or God's favor, but rather to do my best like those who struggled with sin in the Bible.

I Samuel 16:7 says that God sees not as man sees, for man looks at the outward appearance; but the Lord looks at the heart. I pray for all of my brothers and sisters throughout the world who struggle with addictions and habits of sin. When I was younger, sin seemed bigger than my ability to resist it. Sometimes the Lord does amazing and liberating miracles, which set people free in an instant. However this is not always the case. Many times we must confront this struggle head on with Bible reading, prayer, fasting, fellowship, witnessing, and church attendance. In other words, the essential aspects of every Christian life that manifest themselves when we are saved by His grace. I once read that when Billy Graham traveled, he always had an accountability partner with him in an adjacent room. This is not always possible, but looking back I wish I had been as smart as Billy Graham.

Having said all that, on with the story. I was visiting Santa Clara on a weeklong business trip. The company I worked for assigned me a specific hotel with a specific room, which I asked for at the counter. The hotel attendant had her back turned to me and all I could see was her long blonde hair. As she turned toward me, I was staring at the face of the most beautiful woman I have ever seen, and as she saw me she said, "Oh my, you're so handsome."

I'm sorry to say that I was immediately tempted. The woman behind the counter's name was Julie and she asked me if she could come to my room after she got off work. I simply said yes, took my key and suitcase, and went up to my room. Julie visited my room several times while I was in Santa Clara. I was scared, feeling deserving of any punishments that God would inflict upon me. I felt extremely guilty, yet that didn't stop me from sinning. I am still not sure if it was the Holy Spirit convicting me of the sin, or if it was me convicting myself, or if it was Satan, the deceiver, taunting me. At the end of the day it didn't matter. All I know is that I was indulging in sin and it felt horrible in my heart and in my mind.

Whenever Julie would leave my room, I would drop to my knees praying, sobbing to God for forgiveness, and God would comfort me and show me grace. Call it hypocritical or just plain sinful, but I was tormented by what I was doing. I could not stop myself from giving in to the temptation. It felt like I was trapped in that hotel for the week with no escape. I hated myself for sinning and not being able to stop.

One morning, I fell to my knees on the hotel carpet, praying and calling out to God. My spirit was so crushed that I felt suicide was my only option. I couldn't stop sinning, and life was no longer worth living. I couldn't forgive myself for constantly being pulled into sin.

I was on the seventh floor of this hotel; the ground 70-feet below was calling to me. Determined to end my life, I tried every window, but they would not open. I fell back onto my knees and cried out to God for help. Exhausted and afraid, I knelt with tears pouring from my eyes, my heart screaming for forgiveness, I noticed a small cardboard placard next to the hotel phone. It read... "Potential suicide victims, call this number." With tear-filled eyes and snot running from my nose, I crawled across the floor and dialed the number on the placard. An elderly lady with a southern accent answered the phone. I cried out to her:

"I'm going to commit suicide, please help me!"

I will never forget the words she spoke to me. They have stayed with me all of these years. She said, "I was just getting ready to eat breakfast. I just cooked some eggs and they're getting cold."

"Did you hear what I said?" I demanded, "I'm going to die if you don't help me."

"You'll be fine. Just come to our church on Sunday. My husband is the preacher and he's really good," she recited calmly, then telling me the name of the church.

"Are you kidding me? It's only Wednesday!"

"I got to go eat my eggs before they get cold. You'll be fine. Have a nice day."

Click. She hung up.

Obviously, I did not take my life that day. The reason is that I had a new reason to live, that being, I wanted to confront that lady in person so I could yell at her and tell her how inconsiderate and selfish her "Come on Sunday" statement was. I was so mad and crying I decided to find out where that church was so I could go yell at that lady. I got in my rent-a-car, slammed the door and floored the gas, intending to find that lady from the church.

Unable to see with my eyes full of tears I stopped at a college to read my Bible and just cry. Sitting on a concrete bench on the campus, eyes filled with tears, I was approached by what appeared to be a young gang member.

"Excuse me, don't you think it's cool that I'm going to school here instead of gang-banging?"

"Yeah, that's really cool man," I tried to say this coldly so he'd leave, but he didn't.

"I could be writing graffiti on walls, or cruising, or robbing liquor stores, but instead I'm here in college."

I thought to myself, okay, I'll just ignore this guy and maybe he'll go away so I can continue to read my Bible and sulk.

"Excuse me, I could be like my homeboys, out there causing trouble, but I'm here at college instead."

This went on for several more minutes. Suddenly, something my mom said to me years ago came to mind –

"If you want to get rid of someone, just talk to them about Jesus Christ."

So, I thought about it and decided if he said anything else to me I would blast the guy with Jesus-talk. Sure enough, he started talking to me again about going to college instead of gang-banging. So, I laid into the guy loud and hard about Jesus Christ.

"Look, you need Jesus in your life! You need to stop all this bragging about college and start talking about Jesus and how He died on the cross for your sins! And about how you're saved by the blood of Christ! You need to become born again NOW!"

I thought the guy was going to turn and run away from me as fast as he could, but instead, to my surprise, his eyes welled up, and there, next to that bench on that college campus, he said with a loud and very sincere voice,

"I NEED JESUS, PLEASE HELP ME RECEIVE JESUS!"

Utter disbelief and shock overwhelmed me. If you're not a Christian, try to understand that someone passionately asking you to help them receive Jesus into their heart is the most honorable pleasure and the most important thing in the world. For this guy to cry out to help him receive Jesus was a miracle. God truly showed me His love in that moment. He knew how to snap me out of my guilt and emotional pain. He knew how to love me. I believe to this day that this was no coincidence. This was God's divine plan. This man wanted and needed Jesus in his life.

As we stood there together, I asked his name and he said it was Jose. I lead Jose in the sinner's prayer and he received Jesus into his heart and was crying sincerely for mercy and grace.

"Silver, I'm not sure what just happened when I said that prayer but my eyes have been opened. All of the stories I was taught in Catholic school as a young boy suddenly make sense now."

"What do you mean?"

"I never understood those stories before. When I said that prayer, I now understand. For instance, when Jesus was taken to the top of the mountain and Satan offered Him all of the kingdoms of the world for one act of worship, Jesus said 'You shall only worship the Lord your God.' I now understand that I was being offered the riches of this world if I would bow down to them and give my time and my efforts to gain material wealth, when in fact I need to devote my life speaking to these students about Jesus."

I was astonished about Jose's new-found wisdom and insight. We spoke for a long time about Christ and Bible stories that he now understood. He now spoke with a completely different narrative. Now Jose spoke of Christ's crucifixion. He spoke with great beauty. I wrote down Jose's full name, his phone number, and address. I was in awe of God's power; He woke me from my sorrow and opened Jose's eyes in one powerful way.

Later, I was at the airport ready to fly home. I lived hundreds of miles away in Orange County, but, impacted deeply by God's miracle, I couldn't help thinking about how I was going to get Jose plugged into a good church. While at the airport I saved my seat with my old torn up Bible. I got up to go to the water fountain and as I returned, I saw a man flipping through my tattered Bible. As I approached my seat, I looked at the man as if to say, "What are you doing handling my Bible."

He laughed and told me he was a "seasoned Christian" and was just admiring my worn-out Bible. He told me he was on his way to Disneyland in Orange County for the day. Miraculously, this man had the seat right next to me on the plane as well. He said he conducted a Wednesday night Bible study at his house. Both clearly enjoying having another Christian to pass the time with, we talked about God throughout the flight.

While we chatted, another spectacular blessing appeared: I told this Christian brother about the incident with Jose at the college and showed him the paper with Jose's name and address. A surprised looked overcame him when he saw the paper and he said, "Jose is my neighbor! He lives like five houses down from me!"

Once again, God's presence had me astonished. I gave him Jose's phone number and he said he would make sure Jose was well cared for as a young Christian. God is absolutely amazing! I called Jose a few months later to find out how he was. He informed me that he was attending a Bible Study at his neighbor's house and going to church on a regular basis.

Praise the Lord, God is Incredible!

Leaving My Job

~~~

Whether you turn to the right or to the left, your ears will hear a voice behind you, saying, "This is the way; walk in it."
- Isaiah 30:21 (NIV)

I was praying in the break room: "Lord this is a big decision for me, and I've made a big impact at this company. I feel like my time here is up. Please answer me and guide me if I should leave this company or if I should stay."

I was asking God for guidance on whether to leave a certain company where I did work on large mainframes. This same day I sat in my office mulling over my decision when a manager from a different department named Sam came into my office and asked me to walk with him to the warehouse where they stored computer equipment and other large packages. Since Sam and I worked in different departments there was never a reason for me to walk with him into the warehouse.

This was a rather peculiar request but I went with him anyway. As Sam and I walked together into the warehouse I vividly remember noticing how clean and shiny the buffed warehouse floor was and how meticulously the boxes were stacked. I recall thinking, this is obviously a showcase warehouse. As I walked with Sam, I noticed a bright yellow, crumpled up piece of paper rolled up in a ball in the path where I was walking in the middle of the warehouse floor. I remember thinking how out of place this paper looked there in the middle of this immaculate warehouse floor. As I bent down to pick up the crumpled-up piece of paper I noticed some big cursive writing on it. I opened the paper up to see what was written on it and it said:

Leave Here Silver!

I was astonished. This seemed so bizarre considering the fact that I had been praying and asking God to show me if I should leave this company or stay. And miraculously there was this note on some random paper on that perfectly shiny floor. What was even more amazing about that note was that this note was written in my very own, nice, big cursive writing.

Let me repeat that... it was my handwriting on that piece of paper, crumpled up in the middle of the floor of the warehouse that I had never been in before!

Having been invited by the manager that had never invited me to walk with him, I stared in astonishment at that piece of paper in my hand for several minutes just in awe of the miracle that God was performing right before my eyes. I had goosebumps.

I again felt like God was guiding me. I tried thinking logically but all I could think was, this is God performing a miracle. I tried to remember when I had written a note that said: Leave Here Silver. I simply could not remember nor, could I reconcile why I would have even written such a note to myself to "Leave here Silver."

Just then, the manager asked me to carry a computer monitor from the warehouse to his office because he had a bad back. As I approached the computer monitor to carry it for the manager, I noticed a small torn piece of bright yellow paper taped to the front of the monitor with the same tear pattern as the "Leave Here Silver" note.

Suddenly I remembered that several years ago, I had written that note to the warehouse staff so they would leave my monitor there in the warehouse and not remove it. But now, in this moment, God was telling me to "Leave Here Silver!"

A simple note for the warehouse staff had been used by God to show me His direction for my life. Of course, through more prayer and council with guidance from the Bible, I confirmed the choice. However, when it was all said and done, I knew for certain that I was to leave that company.

God shows His love and guidance to us and reveals Himself in many ways. This was just one way He revealed Himself to me. God says in the Bible:

"He who has My commandments and keeps them, it is he who loves Me. And he who loves Me will be loved by My Father, and I will love him and manifest Myself to him."
- John 14:21

God wants to show Himself to you. God wants us to see His miracles. God wants to show us that He is real, and God's revelations often come as rewards to those of us who love Him and follow His commandments. That is what the scriptures say. It would be difficult to find someone that pursues God with all of their heart who has never seen a miracle. Pursue God, be humble, sincere, and diligent about that pursuit, and when God reveals Himself to you, you will never be the same.

Arrogant With Brad

~~~

Do nothing from selfishness or empty conceit, but with humility of mind regard one another as more important than yourselves; do not [merely] look out for your own personal interests, but also for the interests of others.
– Philippians 2:3-4 (NASB)

The church was in a small pink building in one of the lowest income cities in the state, Hawaiian Gardens, California. Pastor Dea Warford preached at the top of his lungs from the pulpit, usually to an audience of elderly, homeless people, and me, a young man in my 20's, handsome, well-dressed and well-built. God called me, I felt, to that poor little pink church for my spiritual growth. Pastor Warford challenged me to meet him for an hour of prayer at 4:00 AM every single morning, and I did. He was a great man of God and a prayer warrior. The most valuable thing he taught me was how to be intimate with God in prayer for an hour every morning, a practice which has changed my life substantially.

I attended that church for many years, but my heart longed to be around other young, single and successful people. I loved the elderly people at the little pink church but at a certain point I began to want something more. I had heard about a very cool church in Laguna Hills, California about 30 miles away, just a few miles from the beach. I was certain that church was filled with young professionals, so I, broke down, moved closer and began attending the singles group on Friday nights. I thought to myself, finally, I'm attending a church where I can meet some cool people. On my first evening there, I pulled into the parking lot and saw BMW's, Mercedes and a few Porsche's and thought this is what I want in a church. I could hear the congenial laughter from the crowd as I rode the elevator up to the second floor. I stepped off the elevator into a big meeting room full of the most beautiful, attractive Christian people I had ever seen, and saw that the things I had heard about this church were true.

He appeared to have something wrong with his arms and hands. Intuition told me that this guy was lonely and looking for a friend. Sadly, I was only thinking of myself and really wanted nothing to do with him. After all, I was there to meet really cool Christians. He limped toward me but I avoided him several times by quickly walking to the other side of the room. This went on for nearly an hour.

Rather than spend the entire evening trying to avoid this disheveled gentleman, I decided to just leave. I strode across the room and got into the elevator and pushed the "door closed" button several times. As the doors began to close I breathed a sigh of relief, but before they were shut completely, a small, crumpled hand slipped between the doors, causing them to reopen. There, in front of me stood the disheveled man. He stepped into the elevator and smiled at me.

"Hi, I'm Brad. What's your name friend?" He asked.

"I'm Silver," I replied. "I'm really busy and don't have time to talk much, that's why I am leaving."

Brad pulled out a small piece of paper and a pencil from his back pocket, and said, "Maybe we can hang out together sometime, bro. What's your number?"

"Look, Brad," I stammered. "I don't have time for any new friends. My day starts at 4:00 AM and I pray at that time for an hour. So, I'm sorry, we can't hang out."

"Can I pray with you at 4:00 AM, Silver?" he asked.

This was about the last thing I wanted. This was my time with God we were talking about. I looked at him and said, "I don't think so. All I do is pray, I don't talk. I don't have time for friends."

"I'll just pray too. I like you and I want to be your friend."

Reluctantly, I gave Brad my phone number. For several weeks straight, he called me promptly at 4:00 AM. Without fail. We'd pray over the phone, every morning for an hour together during those freezing-cold winter weeks.

Sometimes I would see Brad around Laguna Hills, pushing a shopping cart, struggling to walk up a hill. I found out that Brad had Cerebral Palsy and needed that shopping cart to stabilize his balance as he walked. Besides prayer, Brad would call me sometimes, but I would ignore his calls.

One frigid morning, Brad called me at 4:00 AM and as always we began praying. "Brad, I need to call you back in a little while, what's your phone number?" I needed to get some water.

"I don't know what the phone number is here," he said.

"You don't know your own phone number?" I asked, puzzled.

"I don't have a phone Silver," he said.

"How do you call me every morning?"

"I get up at 3:00 AM, get my clothes on, get my shopping cart, and walk up the hill to use the phone in the park."

"Isn't it cold? And why are you walking to the park?"

"Because I want to pray with you Silver, and because we're friends."

My heart broke as I felt the warm tears slide down my cheek. I couldn't believe this man with all his challenges was hobbling up that hill just to pray with me on the phone while I laid in bed! This was one of the most humbling things that has ever moved my heart. I made some comment about how he didn't need to do this. He said he did it because our friendship mattered to him. We left it there, and began praying. After our prayer I felt I needed to tell him that I didn't want him walking to the park on my account. It was too cold and I didn't believe I could take the weight of the situation, so I suggested that we stop praying together until a later date.

Months passed. I started dating a beautiful woman named Dana who soon became my fiancé. I was excited for my upcoming wedding, however, I was now faced with a very difficult decision: I had to select a best man from one of my four brothers. All of them were insistent on being the chosen brother so I had no idea how I would decide. None of them were happy that I could not choose one of them immediately. For various reasons, each of them thought I was somehow obligated to select them. This dilemma made me very anxious. I was certain that if I picked one of my brothers, the other three would react negatively, stop talking to me, and perhaps not even show up at the wedding. That's how dysfunctional my family can be at times and I knew that's what I'd be dealing with.

I made many tough life-decisions while kneeling in the closet, and this one was no different. I brought my dilemma to God and fervently prayed that He help me select a best man among my brothers. I grew up speaking to God, so I knew how to listen for His voice. He tends to choreograph a scenario while I kneel there with my eyes closed. Quietly upon my knees God began to show me a motion picture of my wedding day. It was an absolutely beautiful outdoor wedding in Palos Verdes Estates with gorgeous flowers and ribbon everywhere. My wife was going to be stunning. As the crowd eagerly waited for the entrance of my amazing bride, the camera in my mind slowly shifted to me standing there facing the crowd with my black tuxedo and a brilliant smile next to my best man...Brad!

I was taken aback, but certain that this was who God had selected. I tried to dismiss this as a mistake, but God repeatedly showed me Brad standing with me. When I finally stopped arguing with God on my knees, He gave me peace. At that moment, I knew it was the right decision and I knew it was from God.

Later that day, I got my brothers together and introduced them to my friend Brad. I told them that Brad was going to be my best man. Brad himself was ecstatic, honored even. My brothers applauded my decision and said they were proud of me. God is so amazing. If you spend enough time in quiet prayer with Him, He will speak to your heart or choreograph a picture in your mind to let you know what direction to go. God makes great decisions. I can always tell when it's God making the decision because He tends to provide answers I would never think of myself. God chose a best man that made everyone happy. That is just another way that God shows His love.

Richard The Homeless Man

~~~

But those who wait on the LORD shall renew [their] strength; they shall mount up with wings like eagles, they shall run and not be weary, they shall walk and not faint.
– Isaiah 40:31

Richard was his name, a homeless man standing next to the freeway holding up a cardboard sign asking for money. He was disheveled and appeared to be living on the streets for many years. I pulled over and asked him if he would like to have lunch with me. He was very grateful and hopped into my car. Richard was probably in his early 40's, about 6'2", built like a truck with long hair past his shoulders, and a tattered beard. He was filthy from living on the streets and as you can imagine, he smelled really bad.

We walked into a café and as we ate together, I asked Richard to share his story of how he ended up on the street. He began, stifling some tears:

"I started with dozens of friends, a great job, and a great place to live, and I drank myself straight into isolation and poverty."

When we were done eating, I asked Richard if he would like a new start in life. He said he very much would, and that was all it took to invoke me to action. I purchased Richard a membership to the YMCA so he could shower. I took him to buy some new clothes, get a haircut and a shave. I was impressed by the fact that Richard was willing to completely shave off his thick beard and mustache and cut his long straggly hair short. As the hair fell from his face and head and hit the floor of the salon, I noticed that the women in the salon were starting to giggle, looking at how handsome Richard was. Richard was being transformed right before our eyes. This once homeless straggly and dirty man was actually tall, had beautiful bright green eyes, and a smile that lit up the room. I watched as Richard transformed on the outside into this handsome figure of a man.

Richard accepted Christ as his Lord and Savior and started attending church on a regular basis. We even found him a job and a place to stay. I felt proud watching his spiritual growth. As we grew closer as friends, I requested one thing and one thing only from him: that he not ask me for cash. I helped him by buying groceries and helped with other necessities, but I feared that if I gave him cash, that he would start drinking again. Several months went by and Richard seemed to have re-established his life. Praise the Lord!

One morning at 3:00AM, several months later, my phone rang. It was Richard, asking for my help. I got in my car, drove to the bad part of Long Beach, and began to search for him. When I found Richard, he was dirty and drunk, laying on the cold sidewalk on a street corner. He asked me to give him some cash and I said to him, "Richard, our agreement was that you would not ask for cash and I would not give you cash." I offered to get him a room for the night and food, but he kept insisting, in a loud and indignant voice that I give him money.

After I told him no several times, Richard eventually curled up into a little ball on the cold sidewalk and said, "Just leave me alone." I wept in my car for a long time and eventually drove home. I never saw him again after that. When I left, he was once again cold, drunk, dirty and alone. It was such a sad and disappointing moment seeing months of Christ's work in Richards' life turned to dust. Sometimes we feel like all we've done in some circumstance is for naught: That is how I felt at that moment.

Ten years later, I got a call from an old psychology professor friend of mine, Professor George Ampudia. After catching up for a bit, he said, "Silver, I was lecturing to one of my classes recently and I brought up your name to talk about your tough childhood. After class one of my best students approached me and asked me, 'Did you say you knew someone named Silver Fisher?' I said 'Yes. I know Silver Fisher, he's a friend of mine' and my student said, 'I know Silver Fisher too! Fifteen years ago, I was an alcoholic living on the streets of Long Beach, and Silver Fisher helped me get sober and get my life together. I'm a changed man today because of Silver's help.'"

Professor Ampudia went on to tell me what a successful life Richard was now leading and how much he appreciated what I had done for him. Professor Ampudia said that Richard was a good business man and one of his best students. What a transformation from when I had last seen him! That poor man laying on the curb begging for money hadn't finished that way. Through God's grace Richard was able to clean himself up again and make a better life for himself. Sometimes we don't get to see the end result of God's final product, but it is awesome when we do. I was blessed by the testimony and it taught me a huge lesson.

Never assume God's story is done. God can turn any situation around and He does it quite often. God purposely had Professor Ampudia share with me about Richard. God loves us in amazing ways! From that day forward I try not to presume God is done in a situation. The Bible says that as Christians we walk by faith and not by sight. Richard went on to be a success and I grew in faith. That is how God works, He changes the circumstances, the people around us and He changes us as well.

The German Hiker

~~~

"But seek first the kingdom of God and His righteousness, and all these things shall be added to you."
- Matthew 6:33

One time some friends and I were hiking in Yosemite Park. We had just hiked all the way up El Capitan with 50-pound backpacks on our backs. When we reached the top, we unpacked and rested in the cool shade underneath the trees. I recall it was a good hike and I was content to rest and relax.

I walked around a bit and noticed a young guy around 25-years old sitting underneath a tree staring in wonderment at the beauty surrounding him. I approached him and introduced myself. He returned the pleasantries and said his name was Conrad. I asked him if he knew Jesus.

A look of excitement came over Conrad's face. Then he immediately pulled a small New Testament out of his back pocket and said something in another language. I touched his Bible and said, "I don't understand what you are saying, but are you a Christian?"

He very excitedly answered me in broken English and a strong German accent:

"I come here to the top of this mountain to seek for God! To see if He is real or not. I ask God to show me if He is real. I come to ask God if He is real. I bring this little book that someone give me. I tried to read but, I do not understand this book."

I was amazed at God's timing. I knew the Bible really well so I proceeded to open his little New Testament to show him some scriptures about what it meant to be a born-again Christian and to be saved. However, when I opened his little New Testament to show him some scriptures, I was surprised to find that it was written in German.

Allow me to take a slight detour from the story for a moment. My car stereo had been stolen out of my car many years prior to this and instead of replacing my car stereo, I took up memorizing scriptures instead. I have memorized over 100 scriptures. I am so glad I memorized those scriptures because I was able to look into Conrad's German Bible and determine exactly where to show him to read. I pointed to 1 John 5:11-13 which reads:

"And the testimony is this, that God has given us eternal life, and this life is in His Son. He who has the Son has the life; he who does not have the Son of God does not have the life. These things I have written to you who believe in the name of the Son of God, so that you may KNOW that you have eternal life."
- 1 John 5:11-13 (NASB)

This was a great scripture to show Conrad because this scripture says how you can KNOW that you have eternal life.

I showed him Romans 10:9-10 which reads:

"If you confess with your mouth the Lord Jesus and believe in your heart that God has raised Him from the dead, you will be saved. For with the heart one believes unto righteousness, and with the mouth confession is made unto salvation."

Finally, I showed him Revelation 3:20:

"Behold, I stand at the door and knock. If anyone hears My voice and opens the door, I will come in to him and dine with him, and he with Me."

The Bible says there is joy in the presence of God's angels over one sinner who repents. Conrad received Jesus into his heart that day on the mountain. What a tremendous day in Conrad's life, in my life, and in heaven. Conrad went to that mountain to seek God. He had asked God to show Himself to him if He was real, and God prompted me in my heart to ask Conrad a simple question.

All I can say is, learn the voice of God and when He speaks, do what He says. God shows me His love by giving us the privilege of bringing others to Christ. God knows this is what excites me and, like a gift from heaven, shows me His love by giving me these opportunities.

Teaching The Handicapped

~~~

Then Jesus said to His host, "When you give a luncheon or dinner, do not invite your friends, your brothers or sisters, your relatives, or your rich neighbors; if you do, they may invite you back and so you will be repaid. But when you give a banquet, invite the poor, the crippled, the lame, the blind, and you will be blessed. Although they cannot repay you, you will be repaid at the resurrection of the righteous."
– Luke 14:12-14 (NIV)

Bertha's hand held mine loosely, but it was warm, her other palm resting on her wheelchair wheel, which stuck out from beside the pew. She smiled, her eyes rolling back toward me. I used to hold her hand to comfort her during church service, her and her friend Iliff, who also sat, wheelchair bound, next to her. It was hard to understand either of them when they spoke, but we enjoyed rejoicing in the spirit of Christ together, which, when it comes down to it, requires few words. My heart went out to them. I prayed with them often and showed them God's love by hugging them a lot. One Sunday, Bertha gave me her address asking me if I'd like to share God's word at the assisted living home where she lived.

I was still a relatively new Christian and I had an intense desire in my heart to teach the Bible, so I decided that I would visit. A five-foot statue of a Roman soldier stood in the front yard of the home built as part of an older community in Paramount, California. The statue made me wonder about the people that occupied this place.

I knocked on the door and a man opened asking what we wanted. I told him, "My name is Silver, this is my wife Dana, and this is my son little Silver. We would like to teach a Bible study here." The man immediately shut the door.

I was shaken by his disregard to my request and more than a little disappointed in God that He would allow someone to close the door on us without so much as an explanation or goodbye. As we turned to go to our car, I decided to pray with my family as a good example to my son little Silver. Ever faithful, little Silver encouraged me to go back and try again. I didn't want to, my soul slightly defeated already, but for the sake of my son, I agreed to go back and try again. I prepared my heart for another round of disappointment and knocked on the door.

The same man answered and asked what I wanted. I once

again said, "My name is Silver, this is my wife Dana and this is my son little Silver. We would like to teach a Bible study here."

The man replied, "I closed the door the first time because I believed you came here to make fun of us."

I stood there in front of him, unsure of what he meant and asked, "What makes you think I would make fun of you?"

His reply stunned us. He turned to his family and said to us, "Because MY name is Silver and this is my wife, Dana, and this is our son, Little Silver."

For a moment, we stood in silent disbelief, just staring at one another. Disbelief turned into laughter and we hugged each other in amazement. After we confirmed that we all genuinely had the same exact names, joy lit up our faces as we praised God together. God brought us all together in this place. We discovered that they too were Christians. Silver said, "This is a state-funded nursing home and we are not allowed to have Bible studies. However, who can deny this miracle of God? I'll gather the people."

I had faith that this was an absolute miracle, it was impossible to deny. All the right ingredients were present: Prayer, Bible study, two Silver's, two Dana's and two little Silver's, combined with me ready to give my very first Bible study to a room full of eager people... or so I thought. This had God's handiwork written all over it.

As the people began to filter in and walk into the front area where I was going to give the Bible study, I began to feel nervous. I could see ropes hanging from the ceiling that the people held onto for stability as they slowly stumbled in. There in front of me were the most indescribable assortment of handicapped people I had ever seen. Many could not control their bodies and they moved their heads erratically, some were in wheelchairs, like Bertha and Illif, and some others were rolled in on gurneys. So much bodily pain and so many people with ailments, people slumped over in their wheelchairs, some unable to speak, some with bladder control issues and others shaking their heads uncontrollably.

The environment was clean and tidy, but the odor was very strong. I cried and my heart melted as I looked at the people in the growing crowd before me. When they had all gathered and the room was completely full, I knew I was not prepared nor capable of teaching this group of people, but I was there to do God's work and I wanted to do my best.

Unprepared for this impromptu Bible study I began to teach about Adam and Eve and I quickly saw that they did not understand the story. I almost cried and wanted to run out the door because I didn't know what I was going to do. I bowed my head and asked God to guide me. I silently prayed "Lord, I don't know what to do, but my eyes are on You and I'm asking for Your help please." I began to feel the presence of God. God spoke to my heart and said to me, "Tell them to praise Me and give Me thanks." Under my breath, I quietly began to argue with God thinking, what do these people have to be thankful for, what reason do they have to praise You?

With no other choice before me I obeyed God, I said with a very loud voice, "Lift your hands in the air like this, praise God and tell God you love Him and give God thanks!" All at once, their voices began to burst into loud laughter and praises, thanking God uncontrollably with great joy and with hands lifted high in the air. They continued to praise God and thanked Him over and over again. Praise filled the air of that room, they were rejoicing hard and laughter echoed off the walls. I could see some of the people in their wheelchairs with arms flailing in the air lifted high, and those holding on to a rope with one hand and lifting the other hand to God. They praised the God of the heavens uncontrollably over and over again.

We were witnessing a miracle. I was part of this amazing miracle of God. I remember knowing that God was present performing one of His outstanding and unique miracles in that room as all of us cried and praised God together. The praise continued, even when I tried to get them to stop. They would not. They loved praising God! There was no music, no inspirational sermon, no praise band, just all of us giving thanksgiving, praying, worshiping and praising God Almighty. I was astounded and overtaken by deep emotion watching these blessed people.

They were praising God with all their hearts for His greatness and for all He had done for them. Wow! I looked over at the other Silver, the two Dana's and little Silver's and we all had tears in our eyes as we watched in awe!

It was clear to all of us at that moment that God was present and that He wanted us to know what it says in the Bible in Luke 19:40 when Jesus said:

"I tell you that if these should keep silent, the stones would immediately cry out."

Who Am I?

~~~

As for the saints who [are] on the earth, they are the excellent ones, in whom is all my delight.
-Psalm 16:3

I love to pray! Many times, I have sought God in quiet reverence. I often pray on my knees surrounded by my Bible, a pad of paper, a pen, and a dictionary. I keep the pad of paper while praying just in case God chooses to speak to me. My dictionary has come in handy many times when I read the Bible on my knees and I read a word that I don't understand.

I began to pray one day for God to help me understand more about myself and how I look in His eyes and the eyes of others around me. This was a time of self-introspection and I needed to know these things from God. So, I bowed my head humbly and listened for God's voice to speak to my heart about who I was, but God's voice never came. After a long time upon my knees, I finally gave up on asking God who I was. Instead, I began randomly reading through my Bible upon my knees.

As I read through my Bible, I came across the word "sovereign." I didn't know the meaning of the word sovereign, so I flipped open my dictionary to the letter S. Have you ever opened a book to the exact page you wanted? Well, that's what happened to me that day, on my knees. I flipped open my dictionary to the exact page that I needed. However, I didn't find the word 'sovereign' at the top of the page but the word SILVER! I thought that was miraculous. Here I am asking God to show me who I am, and there staring back at me in black and white from the pages of my dictionary is the word Silver.

My name is Silver Fisher. When things like this happen, especially when I'm on my knees praying, I always know it's a miracle sent to me by God. I do not run around telling everyone that I have witnessed a miracle, but I know in my heart that God is speaking directly to me. God was definitely speaking to me.

In all my years on this earth, I had never thought to look up my name in the dictionary. I'll admit, it was pretty exciting to see. I began to read the definition and the meaning brought surprise to my heart. It read something like this:

Silver - the greatest conduit of energy and electricity on the planet.

I was ecstatic! If you know me, I am full of energy and always smiling. I've been told many times that I have an electric personality by my friends and co-workers due to my constant smile and because I'm always shaking people's hands or hugging them. This definition fit me perfectly and completely! I was so excited. I said, "Lord, You are so very cool," and I began to praise Him on my knees, with my hands lifted in the air, and my heart full of joy.

I was enjoying the moment alone with God because He showed me who I am by simply having me open my dictionary. Silver is the greatest conduit of energy and electricity on the planet. This was God speaking directly to my heart from the dictionary and I gladly received that definition of myself.

After several minutes of rejoicing, I went to close the dictionary and I noticed the very next word below Silver was the word: "silverfish". Once again, my name is Silver Fisher and all my life, even as an adult, people have constantly teased me and made references to the term 'Silver Fish'. Here I kneeled, praying, seeking a word from God and not one, but two miracles happen right before my eyes. First the definition of Silver, and now the very next word is "silverfish." I wanted to just close the dictionary, but I never want to ignore a coincidence or miracle in the making, especially while I'm on my knees praying. I was reluctant because I had already received a favorable definition of who I am. Now, I was faced with a small dilemma.

I decided to read further and see what the definition for "silverfish" was. Staring at me from the page were these shocking words:

Silverfish - A small wingless insect, usually a nuisance to man.

I was bewildered. I looked up to the heavens several times saying, "Lord, which one am I? Am I, the greatest conduit of energy and electricity on the planet or a nuisance to man?"

I knew God was speaking to me about something because, in my life coincidences don't just happen when you are on your knees praying. These times have significant meaning. I remember just silencing my inner thoughts and getting very quiet in my heart and mind. As I knelt there in silence I said quietly, God I am ready to receive whatever you have for me at this moment.

The Lord spoke to my heart and said, "Silver, YOU MUST CHOOSE WHO YOU ARE EVERY SINGLE DAY."

That was enough for me. God does not need to speak a lot for me to get the message. Yes, I get to choose every day whether I will be the greatest conduit of electricity and energy, or a nuisance to people. It is not all about God doing everything for us. We have the right and obligation to make those decisions; decisions about who you are and who you are going to be in every circumstance presented to you in your life.

God gives you a choice between blessings and life (received by obeying His will by faith in Jesus Christ) or curses and death (received by obeying our own will in self-righteousness).

Always choose life and blessings.

Always choose to walk by faith in Jesus Christ, which is the only way to be a blessing to anyone.

As for me, I choose to be the greatest conduit of energy and electricity every single day – walking by the Spirit of God through faith in Jesus Christ.

How Should I Live?

~~~

"Then they cried out to the LORD in their trouble, [and] He delivered them out of their distresses... For He satisfies the longing soul, and fills the hungry soul with goodness.
– Psalm 107:6, 9

While married, I wrongly thought that since I wasn't like my dad, brutal and physically abusive, that meant I was a good husband. The truth of the matter is, I was still controlling and manipulative. My father's dysfunction still burned inside of me, but I manifested it in a different way. If I didn't get my way, I would simply leave for long periods of time, a habit I deeply regret. After we were married for about three years, Dana was pregnant and we felt so happy and blessed. While our baby was still inside Dana we named her Mia-Marlette Fisher. Half way through the pregnancy the doctors determined that our little unborn Mia-Marlette had a rare birth defect. Dana and I cried and prayed endlessly together. We were distraught and rightly so, this was certainly the toughest times we ever went through as a family. Months and months of sleepless nights, doctors' appointments and work, our marriage began to fall apart. I remember just pleading with God, trying to surrender, asking Him to help me fix things. I learned to walk with God through this difficult time.

Dana and I had an agreement that when we were not speaking to each other because it was too difficult instead of saying the words "I LOVE YOU," we would simply squeeze each other's hand three times one for each word:

I-LOVE-YOU.

There were many times when we would get so upset at each other but we still loved each other very much. During those times we could simply squeeze three times to say: I-LOVE-YOU.

We tried counseling, which provided us with a description of our problem but no real way to resolve it. I was still very broken-hearted and desperate for answers. I loved my wife, and missed the times when we were closer.

One day as I was driving alone in my car on my way to our

counseling session, I turned on my radio to a Christian station where a preacher named Chuck Smith was preaching. As I prayed and intensely listened, I asked God to help me understand how and whom I was supposed to be in my marriage. As I drove, Chuck Smith said something miraculous. He said, "Whenever my granddaughter and I want to say 'I LOVE YOU,' we squeeze each other's hand three times."

Suddenly, the car in front of me changed lanes and there before my eyes was a brand-new white Mercedes Benz with a license plate that said "BSILVER." I knew God was speaking to me. He was present and I felt it. My real name is Silver Fisher and God has always used my name to let me know He was there. Sometimes the miracles do not need to be big and powerful, earth-shattering miracles for God to get our attention. Just simply knowing He knows our name and that He understands our circumstance and what we are going through is plenty of encouragement.

I knew exactly what God was communicating in this simple but profound miracle. He was saying, hold on to your wife's hand, tell your wife you love her, and be the Christian man that I created you to be. BSILVER!

I drove behind that miracle for about five more miles. I knew God was real, that He loved me very much. During the counseling session, I held my wife's hand and told her I loved her several times. Within the month Mia-Marlette was stillborn. The doctors strongly recommended we mourn by dressing the baby and spending time with her. We laid Mia-Marlette down on a bed, and laid with her, crying and talking to her. It broke my heart to watch Dana fill out the baby-book and answer the questions.

Name: Mia-Marlette, Hair: Brown, Weight: 4 lbs, Eyes: Closed.

Unfortunately, my marriage was falling apart. Dana was moving out small items and was gone several nights a week. The pain of being separated from Dana was too much for me. As I prayed in my closet from sunrise to sundown I ran out of words. Words seemed inadequate to describe the pain of the emotional separation I felt from both Mia-Marlette and Dana.

"But the Spirit Himself helps us in our weakness. For we do not know how to pray as we should but the Spirit of God Himself interceded for us with groans too deep for words"
– Romans 8:26 (NASB)

As I prayed with tears and moaning upon my knees, God granted me a new prayer language. He taught me to use this prayer language when normal words were insufficient to convey my emotional pain. The new language was a soft and humble dialect. I spoke these subtle words and came to a deeper understanding of what it meant to be close to God. I grew spiritually through the toughest time of my life and came to realize that God was showing me Himself in a very new and unique way.

As you go through your tough trials in life be open to God's encouragement, His miracles and His new gifts for your life. He cares for you so very much and will endlessly hug you through these tough times. Psalm 34:17-18 says,

"[The righteous] cry out, and the LORD hears, and delivers them out of all their troubles. The LORD [is] near to those who have a broken heart, and saves such as have a contrite spirit."

Living In My Car

~~~

That the genuineness of your faith,
[being] much more precious than gold
that perishes, though it is tested by fire,
may be found to praise, honor, and glory
at the revelation of Jesus Christ.
– 1 Peter 1:7

I stumbled back to the condo from the grocery store, just having bought a few items to hold me over, nothing more. When I entered I noticed that the refrigerator was gone, nothing but a weird lonely coil hanging from the wall. First it was her bags, small items, then some decorations that I may not have ever liked, then the table. Now this. Her and her brother had waited until I'd left. Staying in that place was becoming like living in an abandoned building.

When Dana finally left for good, I prayed even harder. From sun up to sun down, I asked God to bring her back. I learned to bow before the Lord's throne but the pain only seemed to get deeper. I remember having intimate visions of Christ and I walking together in heaven, feeling drops of light rain upon my face, smelling the fragrance of flowers growing out of the cliffs of heaven. I prayed intimately with God every day for weeks. I drew so close to Him that when I was done praying for hours I would leave the closet, stand in front of the mirror glowing, crying but smiling all at the same time. God and I were getting so intimate and so close.

The condo was getting expensive, with only me paying the mortgage. I decided it was time to move out, so I rented it and began living in my car..

My visitation with Little Silver was every other weekend. We would eat tortillas with ranch while parked in random neighborhoods. We would pray for hours together.

I found out that Little-Silver and I could use a small junior college as our home base to brush our teeth and hang out in the Cypress College library. We'd leaf through books and dawdle around the campus. One morning we drove a half-block from the neighborhood to the campus, squinting as we exited the SUV looking rather disheveled I'm sure. As we walked toward the college locker room to brush our teeth and comb our hair we were approached by a campus security guard. He asked me if I was a student on the campus, and I told him no. He told me that we couldn't use the college facilities unless I was a registered student. I came back a couple days later and registered for a class so we could use the school facilities.

The semester had already begun and there was only one course available - Speech 101. If my memory serves me correctly, my GPA during my senior year of high school was around 1.6. I had zero desire to give speeches or even to register for this speech class. I had no interest in speaking, but we needed to use the college facilities to wash up while we lived in the car.

I was broken-hearted slumped over in a classroom with these students seemingly half my age. The professor was a beautiful Hawaiian lady with a big smile and she made an announcement that there was going to be this upcoming speech tournament at Northridge College, and that anyone who participated in it would be able to replace a "C" grade with an "A" grade. Personally, I didn't have any interest in this speech tournament, but I was intrigued by the mention that food would be provided.

The professor announced that it was a huge statewide tournament with students attending from colleges as far away as San Francisco and San Diego. In terms of placing in this tournament, absolutely nothing would be expected of us since we were only a junior college, and our class was merely Speech 101.

The day before the tournament, the professor asked what my speech would be about. I answered: prayer. I vividly remember the professor's response. She said, "Silver, you are not allowed to speak on prayer! I forbid you to proselytize at this tournament." She continued to tell me that we have a reputation to uphold and she would kick me out of the class if she caught me speaking about prayer or preaching at the speech tournament. She emphatically told me not to mention one word about prayer, but that I could use mediation, if I had to use something of that nature.

I didn't know anything about speeches or about speech competitions. But I did know about prayer. And besides, I didn't have enough time to write a new speech and I needed to attend that tournament so that I could feed my son. I arrived at school and bagged some food for myself and Little Silver. We drove to Northridge College, where the tournament was being held. I can remember seeing all the buses from the different colleges and all of these students everywhere practicing their speeches. It reminded me of the wrestling tournaments that I competed in during high school.

The rules were explained to us. They split our team of five into different categories and put us in different classrooms. We had to present in front of dozens of students and four judges each writing notes on the speakers. We didn't present just once. We were required to do it over and over again, moving from one crowded classroom to another for hours. Each time I spoke, I felt myself standing straighter, being filled with a purpose and conviction. There was something to speaking about prayer after having been through the wringer as I had in the preceding months that made the words come out with passion and conviction. All of the speakers got better and better as we advanced though each round of the competition, and it felt like we were feeding off of each other's energy. I had defied my professor and spoke from my heart about prayer, gaining massive energy in the process.

One phenomenal presenter after another spoke about intense subjects such as nuclear weaponry, poverty, deadly diseases and a host of other topics. Every presenter in their own right, touched the crowd, making them laugh or cry. Their knowledge bases were different, their subjects diverse. Their voices rose and fell as they delivered their speeches. After each round, teammates gathered around each other to encourage one another. I stood alone without any teammates because I was the only student from Cypress College performing a speech to persuade. I kept thinking my professor would eventually step into one of the crowded classrooms and hear my speech or that someone would tell her that I was speaking on prayer. That never happened. I just continued all day with my speech on prayer.

Evening came and we gathered in a large, crowded auditorium packed with great speakers, family, and friends. Each section filled with students from the various schools, supporting the speakers. One category after another was announced and the top finishers were named. They finally got to my category: New Speakers– Speech to Persuade. After handing out several awards. The hair stood up on the back of my neck. The announcer said, "Now for the Superior Speaker Award and first place winner for Speech to Persuade, from Cypress Junior College for his speech on prayer, Mr. Silver Fisher." I shook my head in disbelief, dumbfounded, quickly walked up to the stage and received my award. My professor, surprisingly, ran down the aisle and hugged me saying, "Silver, I knew you could do it!" I was so happy, I just basked in the joy of the moment.

The best part of this miracle wasn't winning the Superior Speaker Award, but in what happened afterward. The following weeks were filled with invitations from other colleges to give my award winning speech. I received calls from small and large colleges, state colleges, and city colleges. I gave my speech in English classes, psychology classes, speech classes, and large auditoriums full of people. God used that opportunity for me to speak about prayer in many secular venues after that. I never asked for money for these speeches, but I did ask that they bring plenty of food to the speaking venues and they gladly complied. The only reason I went to that Northridge College tournament was to get some food for Little Silver and I. God used this experience to feed us for an entire year, and in so doing revealed to me a gift I didn't know I had.

I would have likely never discovered public speaking as my gift had I not gone through the trial of being homeless and needing to use the facilities at Cypress Junior College. Had that security guard not watched us stumble out of my SUV and told me I had to be a student, who knows how that would have changed my life. Sometimes great blessings are born out of the trial of poverty. It has become apparent to me as a public speaker that it is not only the words that we say, but the fire we bring to the alter that sets peoples heart ablaze for Christ.

I believe our greatest gifts may come to light during our darkest times and greatest trials. I did not like living in the back of my SUV. I did not enjoy being homeless.
Moses told God, "Who am I that I should speak to Pharaoh and bring the Israelites out of slavery?... What if they don't listen to me?"

God does not call the prepared. He prepares the called. You may have an amazing talent that you are unaware of, and this talent may only be revealed through your next trial. We are rarely closer to God than when we are going through a trial. Pray and ask God to reveal your talent in your next trial and watch God deliver and reveal and open new doors for you. You will be amazed.

"Who [is] like You, O LORD, among the gods? Who [is] like You, glorious in holiness, fearful in praises, doing wonders?"
– Exodus 15:11

Preaching Hellfire!

~~~

And when His disciples James and John saw [this], they said, "Lord, do You want us to command fire to come down from heaven and consume them, just as Elijah did?" But He turned and rebuked them, and said, "You do not know what manner of spirit you are of. For the Son of Man did not come to destroy men's lives but to save [them]."
- Luke 9:54-56

The first meeting I spoke at was held at a house. There were approximately seven single group members in attendance that night, a small fraction of the total attendance of the megachurch it was affiliated with. I spoke about repentance and seeking God, to which the other singles reacted well. That night, people, including myself, seemed to be refreshed by the ability to seek and praise with passion.

This inspired me. In the following weeks I talked to Jim, the singles group leader about starting a prayer group for the singles on Friday night. I said it would be great to meet weekly on Friday's and spend time with God on our knees. Their response was that, they had tried to have a prayer group once a month for the singles and nobody showed up. They told me the singles group people would only show up for social events, like dances or picnics. He told me I could try if I wanted, but more than likely, no one would show up especially on a Friday night.

I have to admit, this did anger me a bit. How could these people claim their faith and yet not even agree to attend a prayer group? At that point I decided to put together a prayer night, believing that I could get some people to attend. Unfortunately, my prayer event went unannounced at our Sunday gathering.

Come the night of the prayer meeting, there were 3 people who showed up: the homeowner (a nice blonde lady with frizzy hair), a woman named Cathy, and myself. We knelt on the rug in the living room floor, chatting about the Lord, giving our testimonies, smelling the beach air waft in from the open door. I spoke with excitement, but felt emotional pain inside, feeling betrayed that no one had showed up, not having realized that the Lord can work wonders in even the smallest groups.

Right as I was about to suggest we begin praying, we noticed the door open for a stocky blonde woman with powerful blunt features who entered, nodding at each of us in turn and walking to sit on the couch. Looking up at her from the rug, I began introducing the group, straining somewhat, to be excited for this moment.

"Excuse me," the stocky woman piped up. "Who gave you the authority to do this?"

"Uh, sorry, what do you mean?" I replied.

"Who gave you the authority to have this prayer group? You're supposed to get permission to do this," she looked down at me.

"We're just doing what the Bible says to do," I looked at the ground.

"Are you a pastor? Are you a deacon at the church?"

"No..."

"Then who gave you the authority to have this group?" She crossed her arms, turning a bit red.

I asserted, "It's a prayer group. We're just doing what the Bible says to do."

We both paused. Cathy and the homeowner looked at me, waiting for me to say something. I was hurt because only three people showed up and now I'm being ostracized by one of the few attendees. As she and I stared at each other waiting for someone to say something I caught a glimpse of sadness in her eyes.

It was a risk on my part but I said, "Can we pray for you about anything?"

There was another long silence as she stared at me. Then

she looked down and grimaced, before dropping to her knees in tears and saying, "Yes, please pray for me."

We took turns praying for this woman as she cried for several minutes. Soon, we began to pray for each other. We felt the Holy Spirit interceding through us as we prayed and worshipped God together on the floor. After a long time of spiritual intimacy with God I looked up at the woman praying and they all had big smiles on their faces, tears running down their cheeks and the glow of God all over them. They were radiant! We knew we had been touched by the Holy Spirit.

I wanted to capture this moment in everyone's memory so I said to the girls, "Follow me," as I brought them before a large mirror. I wanted them to see what they looked like glowing and smiling with tears. It was a beautiful and exhilarating moment to behold. We all laughed and rejoiced for several minutes. No words needed to be spoken. The reflection in the mirror said it all. If you are a prayer warrior, you understand this moment.

A week later Jim invited me to speak on Sunday to the larger singles group. I was thankful that he had continuously reached out to me in love as a brother in Christ. However, despite the miraculous moment at the Friday prayer meeting, inside my heart, I was still upset that most of the Christians in the singles group seemed unwilling to meet for prayer, but were willing to show up for other activities. It seemed like the more I prayed, the more upset I became about people not showing up for prayer.

With a racing heart I arrived home and indignantly got on my knees and prayed for God to provide me with a sermon about hellfire; something I decided these people needed to hear if they were truly going to seek God. During my prayers God continually spoke to my heart and asked me to speak to the singles group, not about punishment, but about grace. I was startled. I said to God, "Grace?! Really Lord, grace?" I prayed and said, "That is not what they need." God again spoke to my heart and said to me, "Write the sermon on grace." I think for the second time in my life I started arguing with God. I decided to compromise, scribbling furiously while kneeling, writing the larger portion of my sermon on hellfire and only the closing comments on grace.

Sunday morning, I tore my covers off, showered and got ready to drive to church so I could deliver my message on hellfire. I was on the 405 freeway going about 60 mph, gripping the wheel, repeating certain phrases I planned to say. I had my sunroof and windows slightly opened. As I accelerated around a bend, a gust of wind entered my car and carried away a stack of papers I'd laid in the passenger seat. I watched in my rearview mirror as all of my sermon notes flew onto the freeway scattering 'hellfire' to the oncoming cars.

I pulled over to the side of the freeway to figure out what had flown out the window and much to my surprise, all my pages and notes on hellfire and damnation had flown out the window. My sermon on punishment was completely gone! And there, laying neatly and undisturbed on my passenger seat, was one sheet of paper with my closing comments about God's grace.

When I arrived at church, I stood in front of the singles group and testified to the singles group about everything that had happened about wanting to preach on hellfire and how God threw my sermon out of the car window, but left the one sheet of paper about grace. Then something unexpected happened. Everyone in the singles group stood up and started clapping, cheering, slapping high fives and praising God. I stood in front of everyone amazed by their joy over this incident. But what happened after the sermon surprised me even more. The entire singles group immediately started talking about attending the prayer group on Friday nights!

I believe they recognized God's powerful protection, grace, and love for them. This was amazing to me how I wanted to torch them with hellfire, and God wanted to love them with His grace.

Everyone started attending the Friday night prayer group. No Bible study. No instrumental music. No sermon. We just prayed for several hours. We had the greatest time! The group reached over 70 single people showing up to pray and rejoice. It was like a spiritual celebration every Friday night. One time a guest said she didn't know the exact directions how to get there so she just followed the light and the laughter and was able to find it.

God is so awesome. He takes our little feeble way of thinking and turns it into a victory for His glory. I thank God I am a Christian and that God accepts me the way I am. If not for His grace and mercy I would be like those hellfire notes - tossed to and fro into the wind, lost in life, without a Savior. Thank You Jesus!

Fasting And Praying

~~~

"For where two or three are gathered together in My name, I am there in the midst of them."
– Matthew 18:20

Michael David visited my desk, as he often did, to ask me if I knew which production library contained the job control language. This was a typical sort of question I got from newcomers at the company. Michael David was a soft-spoken Asian gentlemen with a poor complexion, who wore suit-pants and a plaid shirt. I answered him, not looking up, banging out green letters on the terminal, telling him the name of the library in a short tone.

"Thank you Mr. Silver," he nodded slightly.

"Don't mention it," I said. Michael David spent some time examining the things on my desk for which I gave him a sideways look.

"Is this your Bible Mr. Silver?" He had flipped open the inside cover of my Bible, which had hundreds of notes in blue, black, and red, starred passages, frayed pages, and cracked binding.

"Yes," I said.

"It's a very nice Bible Mr. Silver. Do you read the Bible a lot?"

"Thank you," I typed a command to mount a disk onto a UCB. "Yeah, I read it every day."

"Thank you Mr. Silver." He left, closing my Bible carefully. I pressed enter, glad the man was gone.

During lunch I followed my usual schedule, walking out to the parking garage to fast and pray in my car. I'd, of late, been longing to share my time in prayer with another person from work; not dissatisfied with my lone pursuit of the Lord, but simply wanting the Spirit to appear in the midst of a few, as the Bible promises. During my prayer time God told me that He had sent a quiet, humble person named Michael David to pray with me. I felt ashamed that this was the guy I had been indifferent towards whenever he came to my desk. The next time Michael David came to my desk I invited him to come and pray with me in my car at lunch.

"But look though man, I'm very disciplined. I don't want to talk. I don't even want to pray out loud. I let God speak to me during this time. There's no food," I explained.

"Mr. Silver, I would be honored," his face opened up.

"I'm not looking for a friend," I began.

"I would be honored, Mr. Silver," he insisted.

I nodded and told him where we should meet the next day. He went off, as I eyed my tattered Bible, closed on my desk. That was the beginning of a daily, month-long routine of sitting in silence, me in the driver seat, Michael David in the passenger, simply spending time with God.

Some time toward the end of that month, it was pouring rain. I was driving on the freeway to pick up a friend of mine that I'd invited to church. My windshield wipers where moving back and forth but it was still hard to see the road. I noticed a car accelerating toward me, really just a blur, stopped in the middle of the freeway. I hit the brakes hard and yelled as I tried to avoid crashing into the stopped car. I felt my car hydroplane forward as I braced for impact. My chest lurched, caught by the seatbelt's rigor mortis, my car hit the other car with full impact as I heard the crunching of steel and breaking glass.

I looked up from my steering wheel and noticed a small Asian lady getting out of her smashed car screaming, "You go to fast!" In the pouring rain other cars swerved around us trying to avoid hitting us. Both of our cars were totaled. I walked the Asian lady to the side of the freeway and called the ambulance. Fortunately, no one was badly injured.

Monday morning Michael David arrived at my desk and said, "Mr. Silver, what shall we do? We have no car to pray in?" My brother had driven me to work. Michael David didn't have a car.

"I'll have to think about that," I said as Michael David shuffled off to his desk.

Our building was a 12 story glass block, with lots of conference rooms, so I thought, there's got to be some place we could pray. I clicked some things on my keyboard, then pressing enter, confirmed my reservation of the 7th floor conference room, thinking it unlikely that anyone would care if we used it during lunch. So, that day we prayed in there, me sitting at the head, Michael David sitting directly to my right, both of our heads bowed, on the laminated wooden surface, accompanied by 18 empty chairs.

"Father thank you for keeping me safe. Thank you for providing us a place to pray," I prayed out loud.

I heard Michael David emoting toward God with his breath.

"Thank you Lord for Michael David. Thank you for his steadfastness in seeking you," I said. "Michael David, you can pray now too if you want," as if I could give that permission to anyone.

This is the point where I would describe Michael David's prayer, if I was enough of a writer to replicate it. I never took the time to consider how close to God he might have been, something that I only understood at that moment. He seemed to feel every word of worship and thanks with his entire soul, spiritually prostrate before God's glory.

We did this for three days, bowing, breathing, and actually now speaking to the Lord before something amazing started to happen. First it was Cathleen from underwriting.

She somehow overheard Michael David and I talking about meeting for prayer and decided to show up. She sat to Michael's right. Then it was Deborah from purchasing, and Margie from legal, who sat on the left. Some days passed and we were joined by Michael from the IT department and Mike from facilities. The group grew - you could even say, exploded, from there, as people from different departments and even different buildings filled the conference room to pray at lunch time.

Michael David often told me, "Mr. Silver, you are a great prayer leader."

The truth of the matter is, there is no greatness besides God's when it comes to prayer, or, really, anything else.

So began the revival in that conference room on the 7th floor of our corporate headquarters. Bible studies happened almost every day of the week. An email Bible message called "The Bread" was started by Mike and quickly accumulated over one thousand recipients. The "Living Bread" was also launched, which was a testimonial time for Christians to share their personal testimony with other believers from the front of the packed conference room. People were bringing guests. People came and got saved. Others came to observe the excitement and enjoy the "church" in this corporation. Lives were being changed, testimonies being shared, backslidden Christians were repenting, and people were being renewed by the hand of God.

I recall one group of Christians having a bonfire at the beach to burn relics of their old sinful lives in the fire. There were people living together who received Christ and got different places to live. People naturally moved into their gifts as we made God, prayer, and obedience the priority of life. God was moving powerfully, undeterred by doctrine or denomination. Charismatic Christians were praying alongside those deemed otherwise; both, of course, equal as children of God. Some people sang, while others read scriptures. Some literally cried out to God and others watched in awe. All could feel the power of God in those corporate prayer meetings. Employees who once saw each other as co-workers now saw each other as brothers and sisters in Christ, truly caring about one another. We saw the power of prayer. We experienced God's presence in new ways and we saw prayers being answered regularly.

When I set my heart to fast and pray, I never imagined that God would perform such a huge miracle! God can work tremendously through situations in your life.

"And they continued steadfastly in the apostles' doctrine and fellowship, in the breaking of bread, and in prayers. Then fear came upon every soul, and many wonders and signs were done through the apostles. Now all who believed were together, and had all things in common, and sold their possessions and goods, and divided them among all, as anyone had need. So continuing daily with one accord in the temple, and breaking bread from house to house, they ate their food with gladness and simplicity of heart, praising God and having favor with all the people. And the Lord added to the church daily those who were being saved."
– Acts 2:42-47

As we fasted and prayed in the car, God did just as He had done in the Book of Acts and increased our numbers. To say this was just a revival would be an understatement. This goes to show that God is all-knowing and all-powerful and can cause such greatness to come out of a bad situation such as a car accident. He is God Almighty and has no limits, no shortages, and no lack of resources to accomplish anything He desires.

They're Trying To Fire Me

~~~

"I will shake all nations, and they shall come to the Desire of All Nations, and I will fill this temple with glory,' says the LORD of hosts. "The silver [is] Mine, and the gold [is] Mine," says the LORD of hosts.
– Haggai 2:7-8

For thus says the LORD of hosts: "He sent Me after glory, to the nations which plunder you; for he who touches you touches the apple of His eye."
– Zechariah 2:8

The corporate revival continued to burn brightly and a new trial in my life was about to occur. The CIO of our corporation decided to combine all of our data centers in the country into one mega-data center in Plano, Texas. This promised to be a huge undertaking, moving the computer hardware and all of the people. It was announced that only one person from our department would stay in Irvine, California, and that all the other operations IT employees would need to move to Dallas or lose their job. We had approximately one month to decide.

I prayed for many nights asking God for guidance and searching endlessly in the Bible for answers to this quandary. This was a huge decision for me and I wanted to make sure I was in God's will since I loved California so much. After much prayer I believed that God was telling me that I should move to Dallas.

My decision came with many trials. I could see that my co-workers began to get very nervous as the decision time came closer. Fast workers got faster. Mean people got meaner. Disgruntled employees got more disgruntled. Laptops and desktops got stolen and competition for that one job in California became the focus of many people. A man by the name of "Big Jed"- a giant man at 6 feet 5 inches and 240 pounds - had the same position I did, and wanted the job in California.

Big Jed was constantly trying to discredit me and make me look bad, at one point, even mounting a campaign with my manager and the human resources department trying to accomplish that goal. I tried to get along with him, but his anger toward me seemed to only get meaner. He even told me once, "I'm going to fire you!"

It didn't take long for his allegations to gain momentum. My current manager and HR became increasingly convinced that I was a lazy, untalented, time-wasting, Bible-reading,

Christian who deserved to be fired. I could see what was happening and asked my manager if I could still move to Dallas, but she said, "No, we don't want to bring problems to Dallas."

I was distraught. I had several meetings with management about my poor performance that Big Jed sent in (keep in mind he wasn't even my boss). I was being falsely accused of praying and reading my Bible when I was supposed to be working. That was just a flat-out lie. I decided I was no longer going to defend myself against the lies. I knew I was a good, God-fearing employee who worked hard.

The next day I was sitting at the console in the data center, when my phone rang. The speaker on the other line indicated that I was needed in a certain conference room. I walk in, and sitting around the table were Big Jed, my manager, someone from HR, and a few other managers. I sat down to a piece of paper which enumerated all of my "slip-ups" from the past weeks. I flipped through and could see that they were lies.

I began crying, saying nothing, staring at this piece of paper, knowing full-well my fate.

"Would you mind if I went to the restroom?"

I went and cried in the restroom, trying to gather myself. When I returned to the conference room, everyone was silent. Someone said, "Okay," then delivered me some papers, after which everyone left. Big Jed's campaign against me had won. The paperwork was done. My manager and the HR department decided that I should be fired the next day.

That evening I prayed outside the corporate office on the cold concrete bench feeling deserted, alone, with no friends and no God. I prayed and cried out for a long time before reaching out for my Bible. Next to where I was sitting was a tiny light I used to read my Bible one scripture at a time. I arbitrarily flipped open my Bible and tilted it toward the light. Staring back at me in that tiny light was one solitary scripture that jumped off the page.

"… The silver is Mine"
– Haggai 2:8

My name is Silver, and this scripture hit me like a Mack truck. Tears ran from my eyes onto the page of my Bible as I read those words over and over again.

The Silver is Mine.

I asked myself if indeed God was speaking to me. I continued to move the Bible so I could read more scriptures under that one tiny light. This is what I read that night.

"Indeed, what have you to do with Me, O Tyre and Sidon, and all the coasts of Philistia? Will you retaliate against Me? But if you retaliate against Me, swiftly and speedily I will return your retaliation upon your own head; because you have taken My SILVER and My gold, and have carried into your temples My prized possessions.."
- Joel 3:4-5

"Be strong… and work, for I am with you," says the Lord of Hosts.
– Haggai 2:4 (paraphrased)

"My Spirit remains among you, do not fear."
– Haggai 2:5 (NASB paraphrased)

"The silver is Mine…"
– Haggai 2:8

"In this place I will give you peace," says the Lord of Hosts
– Haggai 2:9 (paraphrased)

"I will make you like a signet ring, for I have chosen you," says
the Lord of Hosts.
- Haggai 2:23c

"For I,'"declares the LORD, "will be a wall of fire around her,
and I will be the glory in her midst."
– Zechariah 2:5 (NASB)

"For he who touches you touches the apple of My eye."
- Zechariah 2:8c

Considering all of those scriptures that God was showing me in the Bible that night, I felt in my heart like God was saying to me, "How dare they touch My Silver. The Silver is Mine!"

I sobbed like a child knowing that God was present beside me on that bench. I could feel goosebumps on me and I sensed that Big Jed had touched God's "Silver" and "the apple of God's eye." I knew they were going to fire me, but I also realized God was in control and that I could trust Him.

I walked into the computer room where I worked, eyeing the equipment which awaited it's transportation cross-country, knowing this was my last night at this great company. A super nice guy that I worked with named Vince, was working at one of the computer consoles and said, "Did you hear who they put in charge of the entire computer department and in charge of the move to Dallas?"

I said, "No who?"

Vince replied, "Richard."

As it happened, Richard was one of my closest friends. He was a programmer who made some of the jobs I would run as a computer operator. A few times I fixed his programs at night so he wouldn't need to come into work to fix them. Rich had won the President's Award out of 70,000 employees earlier that year, and was on the executive fast track at this Fortune 500 Company. I thought that perhaps I was in for another miracle, however, my stomach was still nervous from the fate of potentially being fired the next day.

The next day when I saw Rich in the computer room, I shared my story with him about Big Jed trying to fire me. Rich said, "I just got out of a meeting about you Silver, and basically you're already fired."

Out of excitement, I said, "Rich you don't understand. God is going to do a miracle through you." I boldly told him about the scriptures God showed me. I told him that God was going to save my job through him.

Rich said, "Silver, there is nothing I can do to save your job. Everything is already done. You're basically fired already. Maybe I can get you a job at another company."

Undaunted, I said, "Rich, you are going to save my job. I know God is performing a miracle in this situation. You were promoted and brought here by God for a purpose. And I read those scriptures under the light one at a time, and that was not a coincidence. I know God and how He works. You are going to save my job."

Miraculously, the next day, human resources called Rich into a meeting and asked him to sign the final papers to fire me. Rich acted like he did not know me and did NOT sign those papers. Instead he said, "If this Silver Fisher guy deserves to be fired, I will decide his fate and I will fire him myself, but I'm not taking someone else's word for it."

That was a very bold move by Rich to deny what they were requesting of him on his very first day on the new job. Rich was always a fair man with a very strong character, and this was one test of his strong character. Rich kept me employed because he understood my value to the data center's move and he had always appreciated my walk with Christ. Thanks to God, ever faithful, I was awarded the one position in California, a big promotion, which came with a 40% raise, which was unprecedented at this company!

Big Jed reacted with angst. He was furious at Rich for saving my job. Big Jed came into the data center full of anger. Thinking me and the new female temp were the only people in the room, Big Jed began to loudly curse about Rich and call him names over and over. He did not realize that Rich's wife had been hired as a temp the day before and she was the person standing next to me. I said, in a soft voice, as he continued to curse about Rich, "Ed, this is Rich's wife." Big Jed was so embarrassed and ashamed that he had been cursing about the new boss Rich in front of his wife and knew this could likely lead to him being fired.

God continued to work miraculously during my tenure at this company. Big Jed found himself in need of prayer for his daughter that had fallen ill, and because of this, he and I became close friends in prayer. My manager who sided with Big Jed was almost fired by the CIO and began to pray and asked for prayer, and became born-again with her entire family. An even larger revival broke out in the company.

God did amazing things, but first and foremost, He showed me that He was there with me through this trial. He did not desert me and He saved my job and promoted me, gave me a 40% raise and prevented me from going to Dallas. He saved several dozen people through the process.

Wow, what an amazing God we serve! I'm humbled, it was a tough trial, but God showed Himself to several of us in the company. If you are in a trial, pray a lot and be encouraged through the miracles God is doing in your life.

My Baby On A Heart Monitor

~~~

Then He said to me, "Do not fear, Daniel, for from the first day that you set your heart to understand, and to humble yourself before your God, your words were heard; and I have come because of your words."
– Daniel 10:12

After my latest trial ended, everything seemed to be going great. Two revivals blazed on, one at my place of work, one at my church; many people, and I grew progressively closer to the Lord. We enjoyed what seemed to be a time of joy and excitement.

As a bonus blessing, my wife and I were going to have a baby! We decided to name him Calvary. There was a moment of peace in the house, but with every step forward, it seemed life, with its trials, was not far behind. We came to find out that Calvary, nearing eight months in the womb, was caught in an awkward position with the umbilical cord wrapped tightly around his neck. The doctor told us that Calvary was in distress inside the womb. They could not perform a cesarean. A natural childbirth would cause Calvary to be choked by the umbilical cord resulting in either brain damage or death.

My wife and I basically just stared at each other, having nothing to communicate except the feeling of fear that our child would not make it. I remembered my experiences with Mia-Marlette, my lost daughter, and desperately wanted to avoid that outcome. We prayed and prayed for Calvary every day. I had spent my life praying, but this felt different, even more urgent.

Calvary was born, very weak, through a miracle birth at the hands of a very experienced surgeon. The prognosis was uncertain. After a week of intensive care, the hospital sent us home with an apnea machine to hook up, monitoring my son's heart rate and breathing at all times. The doctors told us that when Calvary stops breathing, or his heart stops beating, the machine would sound a very loud and hideous alarm. So, every night, we were stunned awake by a loud, frightening alarm, running to Calvary's room, having to shake him to initiate his breathing and heartbeat. A dozen wires were attached to his soft skin.

This went on for several months. Each time that alarm sounded, we prayed that God would restore life to our beautiful son. Poor Calvary hated those wires that were attached to him, and we hated seeing him this way. We were not blessed with a good night's sleep for months. Seeing our baby laying there with all those wires, was so hard. We prayed constantly and rejoiced in our baby Calvary and thanked God that he was alive.

I was asked at one point to preach at a 3-day seminar for an all-Spanish church (I don't speak Spanish, but they said they'd provide an interpreter). Although our full attention as a couple was on making sure our son was well, I accepted the seminar invitation without hesitation, intending to speak to the people about God's miracles in our times of need; something I myself needed to hear.

On the day of the seminar, I told the people, my words being translated, many of the stories of the miracles that God had performed in my life. I told them of my current trial about Calvary's breathing and heartbeat, the blaring alarm, and our constant prayers for his life. I closed the seminar by saying that I didn't know what would happen with our tiny son's life, but that I trusted that God would work a miracle. I was speaking as if I had faith about our situation, but deep down inside I knew I was crying out to God to please help my unbelief, for it was hard not to doubt.

Calvary's doctor, after several months, informed us that an apnea specialist was being flown in from Minnesota to analyze his unique situation. A week later the specialist arrived and examined our son and analyzed his apnea machine output. This took about three days, filled with anticipation and prayer.

"Mr. and Mrs. Fisher I have great news for you. The apnea machine is broken. Your son Calvary is a very healthy baby and he has no breathing or heart problems whatsoever."

The apnea doctor showed me the apnea monitor output saying that it showed that Calvary continued to breathe even after his heart stopped.

"That is impossible. He cannot continue to breath without heart function. This shows me that this apnea monitor is broken, and we will get a new machine to show you what is really happening with Calvary."

They gave us the new apnea monitor and it never, not even once, alarmed. Our beautiful Calvary was healthy!

There are trials we will endure that can be beyond our faith. When a loved one is dying, few can say, "I have great faith." We can encounter trials that are extraordinarily tough. These trials may make us want to curl up into a ball on the floor begging for God to help us and saying, "God, I cannot do this on my own. Please God help me with my unbelief." I wish I could say that God will fix everything, and heal everyone every time, but the truth of the matter is that God has already done that 2,000 years ago on a hill called Calvary, where his Son shed His blood for our sins. That work of God is sufficient for us no matter what happens in our lives now.

A few weeks later, my mother-in-law went into the doctor's office for a backache, and found out that she had stage four cancer of the kidneys. Her last request was that we raise Calvary our son in New Mexico. This was a daunting request which was sure to be fraught with trials.

Last Chance

~~~

The nations will see your righteousness, And all kings your glory; and you will be called by a new name which the mouth of the LORD will designate.
– Isaiah 62:2 (NASB)

Thinning and frail, my mother in law Margaret laid in bed as we prayed for her. We prayerfully decided to honor her request to raise our son Calvary in New Mexico. In so doing, we gave up our prosperous life in California, and moved out to the desert. Life was good in New Mexico for the first couple years. However, our savings eventually depleted and neither of us could find work. The financial burden actually made our marriage stronger, and two years after our move, God blessed us with our beautiful daughter, Makenzie.

Poverty was tough. Our family slept in a one-bedroom apartment with Calvary sleeping on the couch every night and Makenzie shared the bed with her mom. Food was scarce for everyone but we never let the kids know about our scarcity. We often cried as we both got skinnier from not eating, trying to support the kids.

I fervently looked for work, making flyers and submitting resumes at night, and knocking on doors looking for work during the day. A heavy set, green-eyed man named Robert owned a one man business out of his 1974 Toyota truck. Robert would buy products from warehouses and stack the shelves of a few small liquor stores around Albuquerque. He hired me to do the actual work while he collected the money and drove around looking for more business. Sadly, one cold winter night Robert died of a heart attack. I immediately started looking for more work to feed the kids.

I started going to construction sites asking to work for free all day, and then after a full day's work, I would ask them for $20 for the work I had performed. Although I worked hard all day, none of them ever paid me. I just needed the money to feed my kids. As the weeks and months passed I got bolder, having learned that New Mexico was quite different than California.

There were times I would knock on every business door for miles looking for a work. One day, I walked into an older person's office and he tried to kick me out without listening to my sales pitch. I refused to leave and he threatened to call the cops.

I boldly said, "Sir, has anyone ever helped you before? I need to feed my kids! I'm asking for you to please at least listen to me for a couple of minutes."

My life was beginning to spiral downward at a very fast pace. I began to give in to my sinful nature to avoid the mental pain of being financially broke. I was hanging out in the parking lots of some dark and raunchy night clubs. I wouldn't succumb to entering these places but I was there in those parking lots wasting time. For some reason, I felt if I could just stay in the parking lot, watching the drunk women leave at 2 o'clock in the morning, instead of committing any acts of sin, that I was going to be okay. What I failed to realize was that my heart was living in the darkness and running from the light.

God had provided me with several warning signs prior to driving down these sinful streets. He told me I was dabbling in sin, but I chose to ignore God's voice in my heart. These clubs were old run-down night clubs, littered with homeless people, drug addicts, and prostitutes. I didn't know it at the time, but the area I chose to cruise was known as the "War Zone" of New Mexico. I was intimidated and could see that this was not a safe neighborhood, yet I continued to go there.

I drove around this dark and seedy neighborhood and came upon a place called Midnight Bowl. I got out of my car in the Midnight Bowl parking lot and leaned against my car for a while. Alone in that parking lot, I decided I should leave and maybe cruise around. I found another bar a few blocks away where I could better position myself to watch women come in and out of the bar. As I sat in my car, I decided that for the first time, I would go into this place. It was a biker bar. I was not a biker and I didn't know anyone, but the low, intimidating building was calling me to come inside and meet some of the people.

I walked across the parking lot to the back door of the old, dingy bar. Standing before me was an enormous bouncer dressed like a typical biker. He stood about 6'5", weighed what I guess had to be at least 260 pounds, and had a long grey beard. I was well-dressed in some California-type clothes: khaki pants, a pastel shirt, and some multi-colored top-siders, ready to enter the bar. I handed the bouncer my driver's license.

The bouncer said to me, "You can't come in here! Look at the way you're dressed. You're just going to get in trouble here, and I'm going to have to defend you. Go on, and get the hell out of here."

I was completely insulted. In all my life, no one had turned me away for the way I looked. I walked back to my car, my shoulders hanging in defeat. I threw my key on the seat and leaned against my car. I was really angry and decided that I would just go back to Midnight Bowl, the place where I had been previously. Suddenly I noticed two gang members with shaved heads, heavily tattooed and long white T-shirts walking towards me in the parking lot.

They asked me a question in a loud mumbling voice so I said to them, "I didn't hear you." Then they approached closer to me, yelled at me and said, "We weren't talking to you mother*****!" and proceeded to cuss at me. That's when I knew I was in trouble. This was their neighborhood, not mine. Here I was in a dark parking lot behind a biker bar in the middle of the "War Zone" of New Mexico.

Immediately I could clearly hear God's warnings flooding my mind. I was so stupid for not heeding God's previous warnings about my constant dabbling in sin ,and I was about to pay dearly for ignoring God.

The two guys standing before me were real life gang members. One was really big, and the other was short and muscular. Out of nowhere, the short muscular gang member hit me in the face right between my nose and my mouth. I felt the warm blood start to gush from my nose as I bled heavily all over my clothes and the concrete. I thought for a second about fighting back. I was a good wrestler back in high school, but then my inner-voice yelled at me and said, "Don't be stupid! You're losing blood fast. This could cost you your life. RUN!"

And so I began running as fast as I could, bleeding everywhere, my face bloodied and bruised, my clothes soaked with blood. The two gang members chased me. I ran a half-block into the middle of Central Boulevard waiving my arms and trying to flag down the passing cars, hoping that someone would pull over and help me. No one did. Cars started swerving to avoid hitting me. I believe the guys chasing me from the parking lot thought the swerving cars were pulling over to help me, so they turned and ran in the other direction. I watched from the busy street as they jumped into my beautiful Camaro and sped away into the darkness.

Still bleeding, cold and alone, hiding in the shadows afraid that the gang members would come back to kill me, I called 9-1-1 and explained what happened to the dispatcher. I cried out to God, saying, "What just happened to me Lord?" The Albuquerque Police showed up and must have thought I was homeless because I was just laying there on the ground crying.

The police officer walked up to me and said, "Are you Mr. Fisher?" As he asked questions and wrote up his police report, he stopped and looked me square in the eyes and said, "Mr. Fisher you should be happy you're still alive.

Some people just got shot in the parking lot at Midnight Bowl 20 minutes ago."

I was absolutely shocked because that was where I was headed before my assault. As I looked up to cry out to God in heaven, I noticed the name of the biker bar where I was sitting on the curb was called, "THE LAST CHANCE BAR."

I just broke down and started crying again.

"'For I know the thoughts that I think toward you,' says the LORD, 'Thoughts of peace and not of evil, to give you a future and a hope. Then you will call upon Me and go and pray to

Me, and I will listen to you. And you will seek Me and find [Me], when you search for Me with all your heart.'"
– Jeremiah 29:11-13

God wants you to have a good and fruitful life, according to His purposes, His eternal promises, and by the standards of His goodness. I know this, yet I still went out in search of trouble and sin. I was looking to sin that night, and chose my plans over God's on that horrible street in Albuquerque. When you step out of the will of God and into your own, sometimes you will have to suffer the consequences. Our choices can lead us to dealing with consequences that are unpredictable. My car was stolen that night and never recovered. I had a bloody face, ruined clothes, and I could have been killed in the parking lot of Midnight Bowl had I arrived there instead of being beat-up at the Last Chance Bar.

I hope you will join me in appreciation of Jeremiah 29:11-13 and understand that Gods' plans for your life are far better than your own. I should have heeded God's warnings instead of needing to be beaten, bloodied, and almost killed.

I repented from my sin. I asked God's forgiveness. I turned from my sin and stopped hanging out at nightclub parking lots.

Hugging The Homeless

~~~

And my God shall supply all your need according to His riches in glory by Christ Jesus.
- Philippians 4:19

There I was walking, business to business, in the hot New Mexico sun with a suit and tie on pleading for work. In between buildings, I reached into my pocket and pulled out a neatly folded $5 bill. This money needed to somehow feed my kids endlessly. There in my peripheral vision I noticed a dirty and disheveled homeless man with his face in his hands next to a crumbled cardboard sign. I thought that was where I'm was headed if I didn't find some work soon. I walked slowly to the man, sat next to him on the curb, and put my arm on his shoulder.

I said to the man, "Here is five dollars sir."

He lifted his face from his hands and said, "I don't want your money."

I told him, "Here take the five dollars."

And again he told me, "I don't want the money."

I said, "Why not?"

And he said, "You're doing more for me right now than anyone has done for me in years. No one has touched me in years. Please just keep your arm around me."

I put both arms around him and hugged him. I prayed for him placed the $5 next to him on the curb and walked away.

An hour later, I was still knocking on doors looking for work when I entered a very successful real estate office and asked to speak with the owner. The secretary called the owner on the intercom and told him that I was there to see him. A tall, stalwart gentleman looking like a cowboy out of a John Wayne movie, entered the lobby and asked me to step into his office. We politely shook hands and introduced ourselves. Mr. Ingles smiled at me and used the intercom to call his wife into his office. His wife entered the room and looked at me as if surprised to see me. She smiled really big. Both of them acted as if they knew me, yet I didn't recognize either of them.

I asked, "Do you know me or something?"

They stared back at me and asked me, "What can we do for you?"

I said, "I'm looking for work. I can do anything."

Mr. Ingles said, "What would you like to do for us?"

I said, "I can create or improve your website".

Mr. Ingle's responded, "We were at a small intersection today about an hour ago, and we saw you hugging that homeless man in the parking lot. My wife and I are Christians and we want your services or whatever you're selling today. We want to do business with people like you."

Right there in his office, Mr. Ingles wrote me a check for $5,000 to improve his website.

What a blessing! I needed that work and money so bad. I needed that money to feed my family. What did that cost me? It cost me giving my last five dollars to a homeless person, a complete stranger, and showing him compassion and love with a hug. My reaping was more than I could have planned or asked for. Mr. Ingles and his wife blessed me more than they will ever know when they wrote me that check.

I left the office, went out to the parking lot, and cried tears of joy. God is so good and oh so real. Helping others is not an option. It is mandatory for reciprocal blessings in your life. God wants to bless you. God loves it when we give Him a reason to bless us. Be encouraged. The Lord loves you so much that He cannot take His eyes off of you. He seeks to bless you and your entire family. When you are a giver, God will give back to you 10-fold and more.

Honor the LORD with your wealth, with the firstfruits of all your crops; then your barns will be filled to overflowing, and your vats will brim over with new wine..
– Proverbs 3:9-10 (NIV)

Mocking My Name

~~~

I will take you as My people, and I will be your God. Then you shall know that I [am] the LORD your God who brings you out from under the burdens of the Egyptians.
– Exodus 6:7

Weeks later, after successfully completing my work for Mr. Ingles, I again began to knock on business doors looking for more work. I decided to change my tactic from, "looking for a job" to calling myself a "business consultant." I knocked on the door of an old building on a Native American Pueblo, and let them know I was looking for customers. They seemed to be interested in hiring me as a business consultant for their many businesses I promised God from that point on, I would pray out loud in front of everyone In the business meeting before it started. I must admit, most of the tribal leaders did not like me praying out loud because it conflicted with their own spiritual beliefs.

The tribal leaders wanted to have a final meeting to determine if they were going to hire me as a business consultant. Before the meeting, I was informed that the high-priest of the pueblo would be attending this meeting. I was told directly that out of respect, I was not allowed to speak to the high-priest, nor was I allowed to make eye contact with him.

On the day of the tribal council meeting, dozens of tribal leaders started filling the room. I saw the high-priest walk in. He was in his early 50's, a big, handsome man with long, shiny black hair, large broad shoulders, and dark brown skin. I was intimidated, with butterflies in my stomach. The high-priest was a very respected and important man on the pueblo. All of the other leaders met him with silence and bowed heads. I knew it would take a lot of guts and faith for me to pray before the meeting, knowing their high-priest was in the room. After all, this was supposed to be a business meeting where I would present my business consulting services, not a prayer group. I was faithful to God, and as the meeting began, I asked everyone to bow their heads for prayer. I began a long reverent prayer out loud that ended in complete silence from the tribal members.

I started my presentation to show the tribal council my consulting services. The very first slide had my name, and the title of the presentation. As I began to speak about my consulting services, several of the tribal members started mocking me about my name, Silver Fisher. They began to laugh at me. Several of them started calling me Shkaushk, which translated from their native language means, "little silver bug." The leaders burst out in laughter about my name and teased me relentlessly. The laughter in the room got so loud that it made it impossible for me to present. I wanted to tell them why they should hire me and what I would be able to accomplish for their businesses, but their perpetual laughter caused me to be humiliated and my face was starting turn red with embarrassment and frustration.

On the Pueblo, your name is extremely important, and my name was being made a mockery of. In fact, when a new baby is born on the Pueblo, the mother names the baby, then the high-priest gives the baby another name that is considered the baby's destiny. That is how important a name is on the Pueblo. It has a destiny associated with it. My name was destroying my reputation and everyone loudly calling me "the little silver bug" or "Shkaushk," was making me appear weak and useless in their eyes. No matter what I did, I could not keep them from laughing and teasing me. Eventually, almost all the leaders stood up to leave the room. I had barely started my presentation.

I quickly glanced at the high-priest sitting at the back of the room. He had his arms sternly folded as he appeared to be unamused by the situation. In the midst of their laughter and joking about my name, the high-priest stood up and proclaimed with a very strong voice, "Silence! His name is not Shkaushk."

Silence immediately fell upon the entire room and everyone sat back down in respect of the high-priest. Then he said in a quiet but assertive voice, "I give Silver the name Ku-tu-nee."

I could see awe come over the faces of the tribal elders. Several minutes past and no one said a single word, including me. It was if Jesus had calmed the raging sea. Finally, the high-priest stood up and left the room followed by all the tribal leaders in single file, with their heads slightly bowed. Several of them softly touched me as they walked past me leaving the room. I didn't know what was happening, but the silence was deafening as they walked out of the room. I sat there for a while after all of the tribal elders had exited. I felt dejected that I had not even been given the opportunity to present my proposal.

Feeling defeated I pack all of my equipment and paperwork and left the meeting room. With a heart of sadness, I walked toward my car knowing they would not hire me. In the distance, I could see the high-priest walking alone. I knew I was forbidden to speak to him but I had no other choice. I needed to find out what happened in the meeting room and why everyone left when he spoke.

I humbly approached him. With a soft voice and with my eyes toward the ground, I asked him with the utmost respect, "I apologize if I did something wrong, but I just need to know what my new name "Ku-tu-nee" means, and if I can work as a consultant for the Pueblo." In his strong but gentle voice he said to me, "The name I gave you is Ku-tu-nee. It means 'ONE WHO SEES ALL.' It is a God-like status on our Pueblo."

I didn't even know how to say my new name, but it was powerful and full of light. He continued to tell me, "You prayed before the meeting and that was very brave of you. I can tell that you know God very well."

From that time on I was held in high esteem on the Pueblo. They hired me to consult and manage several of their multi-million dollar businesses. My business consulting services expanded on the Pueblo. My company eventually hired many more consultants to keep up with the amount of work that we received. We even helped manage hundreds of employees for them. We led several huge-scale projects and brokered over $84 million dollars on their behalf. I was paid very well for my services over the years as a consultant for the Pueblo. I was so grateful that God had provided for me and my family. The high-priest even allowed me to teach a Bible study at his house and many other Native Americans attended the Bible study. We even became great friends.

"He (Abraham) did not waver at the promise of God through unbelief, but was strengthened in faith, giving glory to God, and being fully convinced that what He had promised He was also able to perform."
– Romans 4:20-21

Before that tribal council meeting began, the thought went through my head not to pray, that it might be disrespectful to the high-priest. I decided that being faithful to God was more important than pleasing man. It was a big risk. I had to have faith. God rewarded me.

God will reward you also when you step out in faith. Please keep the faith no matter what is going on in your life God wants you to have faith and He wants you to have a good attitude no matter what is going on around you. Faith is synonymous with believing that God is in charge. Keep the faith!

My Friend's Marriage

~~~

And they were all filled with the Holy Spirit and began to speak with other tongues, as the Spirit gave them utterance.
– Acts 2:4

There have been many times in my life when my loved ones and I would go through troubled times and our hearts would feel crushed. I would be broken into pieces and would go into my closet to pray for several hours. There were times when I would go in to my prayer closet at sunrise and be in there until sunset. I was broken, yet I felt so very close with God. In my darkest hours, God has always been present. When I cried, I felt Gods' tears upon me and even felt His loving arms reach down from the heavens and hold me. Have you ever been in this place where you can feel God comforting you?

Time seemed to pass so quickly and easily during my time in prayer. There on my knees in that dark closet, I would enter another world where the pain was somehow bearable. I would spend countless hours walking and talking with Jesus, feeling His love surround me and easing my pain. I would envision beautiful waterfalls and tall cliffs lined with colorful flowers. I could smell the wondrous fragrance of heaven and even feel the drops of water upon my face.

Jesus and I would swim together in the cool tranquil waters of the sea of glass. We would converse for hours about my life and His life. My relationship with Jesus became more intimate as the weeks went by and He became my best friend during my trial.

"And before the throne there was a sea of glass like unto crystal..."
– Revelations 4:6a (NASB)

Then things changed. As broken as I was over the separation of my first marriage, I would often become unable to speak to God in my prayer closet. The pain was too much for me to convey words of English to Jesus. Words were unable to describe the pain that I felt because of the emotional separation from my wife. I loved my wife with all my heart. Words were just inadequate to convey the depth of my despair as I tried to pour out my soul to God.

"Likewise the Spirit also helps in our weaknesses. For we do not know what we should pray for as we ought, but the Spirit Himself makes intercession for us with groanings which cannot be uttered."
– Romans 8:26

As I drew closer to God upon my knees, He granted me a new prayer language there in my prayer closet. He taught me to use this prayer language when normal words were insufficient to convey my emotional pain. The new language was a subtle and humble dialect. Softly I would speak these new words and I came to a deeper understanding of what they meant, even though I had never heard or prayed them before. This prayer language transcended and went beyond the incapable words of the English language. It was deeper and from my heart. I could feel emotions being poured out as I left behind the words that I had known my entire life and began to use this new emotional language that God had shown to me.

It was this gift of tongues that was used during my special time alone with God in that closet. I never spoke or prayed this language with other people, nor told anyone about it. This was my time, my language, my connection with God the Father. This communion with God, this gift of the Holy Spirit that I had been given, lead to an amazing miracle in my life ten years later.

I was working as a consultant on a Native American pueblo in New Mexico, and the high-priest of the pueblo, who was also now a great friend of mine, came to me one day utterly broken-hearted. I could see the pain on my friend's face, and I could feel the pain in his heart as he sat before me. This was the kind of pain that cannot be conveyed with simple words. This pain was as deep and hurtful as it comes. The high-priest explained to me that he and his wife of many years had split up. He was broken and humbled by this trial. I could tell that my words of wisdom were not going to help relieve him of his suffering. With tears in his eyes he asked me to please pray for him and his wife to restore their marriage and help him with his emotional pain

In the front seat of his old Chevy truck, the high-priest and I cried together and prayed for God to intercede in his marriage. I knew his pain because I had lived through this type of pain myself. With my deepest sympathy for this humble man, God spoke to my heart and guided me to pray in my God-given prayer language. I knew that the words which I prayed would not be understood by the high-priest but that was of no concern of mine. I was following God's instructions to pray in the language He gave me in my closet many years earlier. I began to pray in a very soft voice in the language of the Lord. When I was done praying, the high-priest said to me, "Silver, I felt a deep peace come over me as you prayed for me. But Silver, where did you learn to pray and speak in Keres?"

I didn't know what he was asking or how to respond to his question. I asked him, "What do you mean 'Keres'?"

He said, "You were just praying in Keres. It is our unwritten native language on the pueblo."

He told me that he and the elders use that language when ceremonially praying in the Kiva. Kivas are square-walled rooms, underground, and are used for spiritual ceremonies. I admitted that I had never shared my prayer language with anyone. He told me that the prayer was beautiful and he understood every word because it was in Keres. I was completely speechless. I was not an elder amongst the Native Americans and was never before introduced to their private spiritual language. This was a gift from God.

As we both sat there amazed at the miracle that had brought the two of us together at sunset, God allowed us to see Him work yet another tremendous miracle through prayer. God was very present in the front seat of that old Chevy truck and in our lives. The high-priest and his wife were rejoined in their marriage shortly after that. God had intervened and healed what mere man would deem as broken and unrepairable.

"For where two or three are gathered together in My name, I am there in the midst of them."
– Matthew 18:20

When God shows up in your life, it will not be in the mundane. Rather, it will be in a way that is heavenly, beyond your imagination, and very powerful. He is God and is not limited by the tangible resources of this world. God loves to bless His children in very creative ways. Keep your eyes open and your heart receptive to the blessings of God. He wants to encourage you and He wants you to feel loved.

I've Lost My Mind!

~~~

Be sober, be vigilant; because your adversary the devil walks about like a roaring lion, seeking whom he may devour.
– 1 Peter 5:8

Things in my life were finally looking up. Once I acquired the pueblo as a customer, everyone in town wanted to do business with us. Acquiring more and more business, I started making great money. I began to replace my time of prayer with time of work, my humility was replaced with arrogance, and my friends went from church people to business people. I bought a beautiful home, new furniture, a $100,000 sports car, and started often cheating on my wife. I'll spare you the emotional roller coaster, and just say straight out: I was sinning a lot.

To make matters worse, I hid my sin from everyone. I continued to attend church and played the part of an innocent "Christian," but like David and Bathsheba, it was only a matter of time before my sins caught up to me. My consulting business fell hard. All of my customers transferred their business to another consulting firm started by my former friend who I taught how to be a consultant. This betrayal was just the beginning of spiritual reciprocation for my sins beginning to unfold.

The fact that I lost all of my customers and money to my friend that once worked for me, left me in anxious desperation. I was still unwilling to admit my sin as my life spiraled further downhill. I soon lost everything, including, my creditability, my business, my house, my cars, my credit, and eventually I lost my memory. Yes, my memory. I couldn't even remember or recognize my wife and my children. My small daughter once walked up to me and I said, "You're so beautiful sweetie, what's your name?" It was as if someone took an eraser to my mind and wiped it clean of every memory. I was traumatically scared. I continued to spiral deeper into memory loss, unsure if I would ever get it back. The scariest part of all was when I tried to pray. I heard several loud voices in my head. It was like the sweet, soft voice of God, which once poured into my heart when I prayed, was now gone. I was so scared, my wife now needed to accompany me everywhere. In my deepest, darkest part of this trial, I did remember one thing: That I had unconfessed sin hidden in the back of my mind. For some reason I knew that confessing my infidelity to my wife and the church was what I needed to do.

This was a horrifying thought that I would need to admit my sin of having an affair, to my wife and to the church. I thought, if my wife left me, I would go insane. But after a month of this trial, I finally gave in to the reality that confession was the only way out.

So, one night I walked into my wife's Bible study, dropped to my knees in front everyone, and said, "I have a confession to make to you. I sinned. I am so sorry to admit this to you and to everyone here. I had an affair behind your back."

I broke down and started vehemently crying and so did my wife. And when we prayed and cried for a long time, I felt this crushing weight come off of me. I went to church the next day, and in front of the pastors and my wife, I once again, admitted my sin and asked for forgiveness. Through several weeks of counseling, my wife forgave me.

God made it so I could go nowhere without my wife by my side. She was assigned by God to help me regain my memory and to make sure we had fun together. She made it fun to re-learn my life skills. She taught me to salsa dance and to go for walks, ride bikes, and act like a kid just having fun. She taught me to appreciate the enjoyment of life. She taught me to slow dance with her before meals, and how to laugh. Perhaps most importantly, she taught me the intimacy of holding hands and hugging. I rather enjoyed my simpler way of life, just being with my wife all of the time. As the stress of sin and guilt was washed away, my memory began to come back. I remembered my wife's name and my children's names. Finally, my memory was fully restored.

After God had done a phenomenal miracle in me and in our

relationship, I learned a valuable lesson to never ever cheat on my wife for the rest of my life. I fear God with honor and respect, and I confess my sins immediately. If you have unconfessed sin in your life, God will forgive you, but until you confess that sin, you will live with the weight that sin carries. Confess your sins today.

Female Prisoners

~~~

"The Spirit of the LORD [is] upon Me, because He has anointed Me to preach the gospel to [the] poor; He has sent Me to heal the brokenhearted, to proclaim liberty to [the] captives and recovery of sight to [the] blind, to set at liberty those who are oppressed..."
- Luke 4:18

Yes, I confessed my sins to God and to my loved ones, to my pastors, and anyone else that would lend me an ear. I cried out for God's mercy and grace and promised to get my life right and never be arrogant and foolish again. I told God I would do anything He required of me to prove my sincerity. God eventually led me out of the mental darkness by leading me to the light of helping other people.

I spent a lot of time at church and they asked me to join a ministry that would lead me to preaching in rescue missions and prisons. I was reluctant, but I followed God's lead week after week. I became accustomed to driving 45-minutes to Estancia Prison with many of my brothers and sisters from the church. On one cold, snowy, winter night, everyone decided to stay at home, instead of going to the prison to teach. It was put upon my heart to go alone. I was fearful to drive alone in the ice and snow all the way into the desert where the prison was, but I knew the desire to go was from God, and so I went.

As I arrived at Estancia Prison, I was greeted by the guards at the front desk area. They told me the men were in lockdown. That means that the men had gotten in trouble and could not attend any activities. I was disappointed that I drove all that way in the snow for 45-minutes only to be told I could not preach. I had driven there for nothing. I turned to leave and the guard asked if I would be interested in preaching to the women inmates instead of the men that evening. I eagerly replied, "Yes! I drove all the way here to be used by God. I'll preach to anyone!"

The guard's question caught me by surprise as Bible studies, and visitors in general, are considered additional work for the night shift guards. We are nuisances because the guards have to open all of the barred gates and escort us everywhere in the prison by opening and closing the barred gates. My escort for the evening was a short, stocky female with a mean, gruff attitude. She led me through several gates and corridors to the place that I would be allowed to preach to the women. I could hear her bark orders on the walkie-talkie as we went from one area to the next:

"Open gate one... close gate one... open gate two... close gate two..." and so on. I attempted to make small talk with the guard, but she didn't want to have anything to do with me. The deeper into the labyrinth of the prison we went, the more my claustrophobia consumed me. We stood at the 7th and final gate and I was about to meet the loud crowd on the other side of the double door.

We walked into this large concrete area surrounded by three levels of prison cells. The room was filled with about forty female inmates who were cussing, yelling and smoking cigarettes. The stereo and TV were blaring out loud rap music and garbled voices coming from the television. The inmates all ignored us. The burley female guard walked over to the TV and the stereo and abruptly shut them both off. Then the guard pointed at me and yelled out above the noise, "This guy wants to talk to you," and she walked out of the room leaving me alone in a locked prison area in front of all of these noisy, cussing female inmates. I stood looking at the forty female inmates for what seemed like a lifetime.

One of them yelled at me, "Turn the radio back on!" This situation had me on my heels, wishing I could be on my knees, praying my way out of there. I felt fearful and alone. This was so different than coming with other Christians where we had an established men's Bible study. I asked myself why I had come to this place all alone. Angry female inmates began to yell and curse at me. The women were too loud for me to even begin to preach, so I just stood there looking at these women ignore me. These women didn't know who I was, didn't know why I was there, didn't want me there, and didn't have a clue about the Bible study. I tried to get the guard's attention on the security cameras to let me out, but no one came. I was getting overwhelmed and honestly, I was very scared.

I had heard about the vulgarity and boldness of the female inmates, but this was way beyond my imagination. One inmate yelled at me and told me to turn around so she could check me out, then yelled out, "What do you want pretty boy?"

I yelled back, "I'm here to teach you about God and to have a Bible study."

The disappointment was very apparent as several of the women then yelled out, "Oh Hell No!" And then ALL at once they stood up and left the area. It was a mass exodus as they all got up at the exact same moment. There I stood, alone in an empty room, just me and my Bible. Once again, I tried to get the attention of the guards on the security cameras, hoping they could read my lips saying, "Please let me out of here."

I was so disappointed and the exit doors remained locked. No one came to my rescue, so I called on God, asking Him what I should do next. As I prayed, something astounding happened: The women all came back into the area with their Bibles in hand and sat down at the concrete tables where they were before. Apparently they had all left to get their Bibles from their prison cells. This showed me the awesomeness of God and I enjoyed every moment of it; until they started whistling at me, making sexual remarks and telling me to, "Preach pretty Boy! And turn around pretty-boy".

I didn't know what I was going to teach about and asked God to guide me. I was very nervous. I never prepared notes because the men were always very easy to teach impromptu. This situation was so very different. I was speechless and saddened that I really had nothing on my mind to say or to teach. The chatter in the room grew louder and louder the longer I waited to speak. I was in a bit of a panic, not knowing what to say, nothing coming to my heart and head. As I looked around the room, I quietly whispered to God, "What should I talk about Lord?"

Then my eyes fell upon a sad and broken young inmate in her early-twenties, sitting in the crowd. She looked just like an older version of my 7-year old daughter Makenzie. She was dressed in a wrinkled old orange jumpsuit. I gazed at this young girl for a moment and was so moved by the thought that this could someday be my daughter. I was mesmerized by that thought then suddenly I realized God was speaking to my heart. God was present and asked me to speak to these women as if I was speaking to my very own daughter Makenzie. God said to me, "These are my daughters Silver. Love them."

I quietly spoke the way I would to my own daughter, "God sent me here to deliver a message to you, and here is the message: I love you so much; I miss you so much; and I forgive you. These walls cannot prevent My love from reaching you, and I AM always with you, even while you are here... I want to take you in My loving arms and hold you. You are My beautiful daughter and I love you so much."

These words flowed from my lips in the first person as God's words moved through me straight to their hearts. I continued to speak to the inmates as if they were my own daughter. The words flowed easily and I could see God's words penetrating their hardened hearts.

As I continued to love them with God's words, I began to hear sniffles and quiet sobs from one after another. Soon there were several women crying. I continued to speak to them, straight from God's warm heart through my lips and now into their broken hearts, healing them. I ministered about the love of our Father God, about forgiveness and with every word, it became easier and easier to give the love of God to these women. It was a miraculous evening there in Estancia Prison.

God delivered an amazing sermon of love and hope straight from His heart to theirs. That night we gathered together to pray an unforgettable and life-changing prayer for all of us. I left that prison knowing God had touched me and the women of Estancia Prison. If you are in an emotional or literal prison tonight, God wants to spiritually set you free, and He wants you to feel the impact of His amazing love. Prisons, walls, or iron gates cannot withhold the love of God from you. The Bible say's God came to shatter the gates of bronze and cut the bars of iron asunder and this message is for you.

I write this book with the same heart and intention that I preached with that night in Estancia Prison.

God says to you:

I love you, I forgive you and I want so much to be your everything. Nothing can hold Me back from loving you...

"See, I have inscribed you on the palms [of My hands]..."
– Isaiah 49:16a

After several years of trials, my relationship with God and my family were back in the full blossoming power of God Almighty. I personally was very satisfied that God and my wife had forgiven me, and that I had a good ministry. However, there was once again, that issue of being financially broke and needing to feed the kids.

Extremely Poor And Hungry

~~~

"Behold, I have refined you, but not as silver; I have tested you in the furnace of affliction."
- Isaiah 48:10

Mike and I stood there warming our hands on a huge open fire with a billion shining stars laid against the black New Mexico sky. Mike and I prayed so hard for God to help us out of our extreme poverty. Mike lived in an old dilapidated, single-wide mobile home with a huge hole in the middle of the floor and no heat. The temperatures dipped below freezing. We were both out of food, money, and no jobs.

Mike admitted to me, "Silver, I tasted gun powder last night." He described how he put the gun in his mouth with the intention of killing himself. He could no longer take the pain of the poverty we were experiencing.

I watched as Mike scrapped around the green mold in the mayonnaise jar to get what was left of the white mayonnaise so he could smear it on his last piece of stale bread. We shared this meal together with hope in our hearts and tears in our eyes. Mike would get angry at God and I would cry a lot in those days. Mike had an idea that he shared with me. He pleaded with me to put his idea on paper and go sell it. I told Mike I was too busy looking for work every day and couldn't afford the time to put his idea on Power Point or on paper.

Through strong assertion, Mike finally convinced me to put his idea on Power Point. We showed the presentation to a few business people, and one of them told us about an investor's symposium meeting in Santa Fe, New Mexico. I made some phone calls and convinced them to allow me to present Mike's idea to the group of investors.

The following week we stepped into a large, beautiful conference, filled with people and a gourmet buffet. One presenter after another approached the podium and presented for 15 minutes apiece. The organizer rang a small bell to say your time was up, then he would abruptly shut off the microphone.

I was the last presenter. Finally, I received the nod from the organizer, an indication that it was my turn to present. I walked to the podium and presented with all of the fervent passion I could conjure-up on an empty stomach. I presented without using all of my time and humbly sat down. The organizer stood up to thank everyone for coming and suddenly, the meeting was over. One elderly gentleman came from the back of the room and introduced himself. He said "I'm Mr. Quintana, I'd like to invest in your company."

He wrote us a check for five hundred-thousand dollars! You read that right - a half a million dollars. God is so powerful! God has unlimited resources. The years of famine and poverty were over in one swift moment. God can break the chains of poverty for generations. He is such an amazing God and He loves you more than you can even imagine.

There may be times, when you think that your burdens are so huge that it will take God a long time to fix them. God is not limited, His resources are abundant, and He is a giving God. He is willing and able to bless you. He loves you and you are His child - forgiven and greatly loved by Him.

"We are hard pressed on every side, but not crushed; perplexed, but not in despair; persecuted, but not abandoned; struck down, but not destroyed. We always carry around in our body the death of Jesus, so that the life of Jesus may also be revealed in our body."
– II Corinthians 4:8-10 (NIV)

But without faith [it is] impossible to please [Him], for he who comes to God must believe that He is, and [that] He is a rewarder of those who diligently seek Him.
– Hebrews 11:6

Epilogue

~~~

Now may the God of hope fill you with all joy and peace in believing, that you may abound in hope by the power of the Holy Spirit.
– Romans 15:13

When I was three years old, my father and I were walking on the sidewalk. I can recall only being able to see my fathers' legs moving back and forth next to me. All at once, with one maneuver, my dad reached down and picked me up and put me on his shoulders. My world opened up and I could immediately see where we were headed. We were heading to the park! As suddenly as my father put me on his shoulders, my view of life completely changed. I could see the many colors of the trees, the gold, red, and green leaves, the green grass, the swings, the red slide and the blue pool. I could see the other kids running around, laughing, playing and enjoying themselves. I was in awe.

Just as I could suddenly see so much more on my father's shoulders, you too can see God's view when you pray and seek Him. The more time we spend in prayer, the more we get God's perspective on life circumstances and blessings. Prayer metaphorically lifts us onto God's shoulders so we can see His big, huge, bright plan for our eternal future. We get to see God's view of our future and what amazing things He has in store for us. Our dull, painful or prosaic life becomes alive with color and vitality, beauty and excitement, when we see God's view of things. My friend, we are headed for something far greater than that park I saw from my dad's shoulders. We are headed for Heaven which human words cannot describe.

But as it is written: "Eye has not seen, nor ear heard, nor have entered into the heart of man the things which God has prepared for those who love Him."
- I Corinthians 2:9

Thank you for reading my life story. There is so much more to my life than these miracles; it is truly one amazing event after another. Thank God I learned lessons through these miracles, but understand, it has always been, and always will be, the grace of God that saves and guides us.

My Favorite Scriptures

~~~

Throughout my life I have seen God's miracles manifested over and over again. The formula for a life filled with God's wonders is simple:

1) Believe in Jesus with all of your heart and confess with your mouth Jesus as Lord;

2) Love one another;

3) Pray a lot;

4) Go to a Bible-teaching church;

5) Fellowship with other Christian believers;

6) Follow God's commandments;

7) Give;

8) Read the Bible.

The entire Bible is powerful and completely necessary to study. Here are some of my favorite Scriptures (some of which have been paraphrased and personalized as God spoke to me) for you to read and meditate on, that have helped me throughout my life.

Genesis 15:1 - I am your shield, your exceedingly great reward.

Exodus 6:7 - I will take you as My people, and I will be your God. Then you shall know that I am the LORD your God who brings you out from under your burdens.

Exodus 9:16 - But indeed for this purpose I have raised you up, that I may show my power in you; and that My name may be declared in all the Earth.

Exodus 14:13 - Stand still, do not be afraid and see the salvation of the LORD which He will accomplish for you today.

Exodus 14:4 - The LORD shall fight for you and you shall hold your peace.

Exodus 15:11 - Who is like you, Oh LORD, glorious in holiness, fearful in praises, doing wonders?

Exodus 34:10 - And God said, "Behold, I make a covenant before all your people. I will do marvels such as have not been done in all the earth nor in any nation; and all the people among whom you are shall see the work of the LORD.

Deuteronomy 1:30 - The LORD your God who goes before you; He will fight for you.

Deuteronomy 3:22 - You must not fear them, for the LORD your God Himself fights for you.

Deuteronomy 7:6 - For you are a holy people to the LORD your God; the LORD your God has chosen you to be a people for Himself, a special Treasure above all the peoples on the face of the earth... Not because you were more in number... But because the LORD loves you. The LORD has brought you out with a mighty hand, and redeemed you from the house of bondage; therefore know that... He is God the faithful God who keeps covenant and mercy for a thousand generations with those who love Him and keep His commandments.

Deuteronomy 8:18 - And you shall remember the LORD your God, for it is He who gives you power to get wealth.

Deuteronomy 9:3- Therefore understand TODAY that the LORD your God is He who goes over before you as a consuming fire.

Deuteronomy 10:12-13 - And now, what does the LORD your God require of you but to fear the LORD your God, to walk in all His ways, and to love Him, to serve the LORD your God with all your heart and with all your soul, and to keep His commandments and statutes.

Deuteronomy 14:2 – For you are a holy people to the LORD your God, and the LORD has chosen you to be a people for Himself, a special treasure above all the peoples who are on the face of the earth.

Deuteronomy 15:4 - For the Lord will greatly bless you in the land which the Lord your God is giving you to possess as an inheritance. Only if you carefully obey the voice of the LORD your God to observe with care all these commandments.

Deuteronomy 23:14 - For the LORD your God walks in the midst of your camp, to deliver you and give your enemies over to you; therefore, your camp shall be holy, that He may see no unclean thing among you and turn away from you.

Deuteronomy 30:9 - The LORD your God will make me abound in all the works of my hands for God will again rejoice over me for good. For the commandments which I command you today is not too mysterious for you, nor is it far off. It is not in heaven... nor is it beyond the sea... but the word is very near you in your heart that you may do it.

Deuteronomy 32:3 - For I proclaim the name of the LORD; ascribe greatness to our God. He is the rock. His work is perfect For all His ways are justice. A God of truth and without injustice; righteous and upright is He.

Deuteronomy 33:26 - There is no one like the God of Silver who rides the heavens to help you. The eternal God is my refuge and underneath are the everlasting arms; He will thrust out the enemy from before me and will say destroy!

Joshua 1:5 - No man shall be able to stand before you all the days of your life; as I was with Moses, so I will be with you. I will not leave you nor forsake you. Only be strong and very courageous...

Joshua 23:3 - You have seen all that the LORD your God has done to all these nations because of you for the LORD your God is He who has fought for you.

Joshua 23:8 - But you shall hold fast to the LORD your God as you have done to this day... For the LORD has driven out great and strong nations, no one has been able to stand against you to this day. One man shall chase a thousand for the LORD your God is He who fights for you. Therefore take careful heed that you love the LORD your God.

Judges 5:20 - They fought from the heavens; the stars from their courses fought against Sisera... Oh my soul march on in strength.

I Samuel 2:7 - The LORD makes poor and makes rich. He brings one low and lifts up another.

II Samuel 7:9 - And I have been with you wherever you have gone and have cut off all your enemies from before you and have made you a great name of the great men who are on the earth.

II Samuel 22:2 - The LORD is my rock and my fortress and my deliverer, The God of my strength in whom I will trust; my shield and the horn of my salvation my stronghold and my refuge; my savior you save me from violence. I will call upon the LORD who is worthy to be praised so shall be saved from my enemies

II Samuel 22:7 - In my distress I called upon the LORD and cried out to my God. He heard my voice from His temple and my cry entered His ears.

II Samuel 22:14 - The LORD thundered from heaven and the most High uttered His voice; He sent out arrows and scattered them lightning bolts and He vanquished them

II Samuel 22:17 - He sent from above. He took me out of many waters; He delivered me from my strong enemy, from those who hated me, for they were too strong for me. They confronted me in the day of my calamity but the LORD was my support. He also brought me out into a broad place. He delivered me because He delighted in me. The LORD rewarded me according to my righteousness. According to the cleanness of my hands ... for I have kept the ways of the LORD and have not wickedly departed from my God

II Samuel 22:29 - For you are my lamp oh LORD; the LORD shall enlighten my darkness, for by you I can run against a troop; by my God I can leap over a wall. He is a shield to all who trust in Him

II Samuel 22:33 - God is my strength and power, and He makes my way perfect. He makes my feet like the feet of a deer and sets me on high places

II Samuel 22:36 - Your gentleness has made me great. You enlarged my path under me so my feet did not slip. For you have armed me with strength for the battle you have subdued under me those who rose against me

I Kings 3:12 - I have given you a wise and understanding heart, and I have also given you what you have not asked both riches and honor...

II Kings 6:16 - So he answered – Do not fear for these are who are with us are more than those who are with them and Elisha prayed and said LORD I pray open his eyes that he may see. Then the LORD opened the eyes of the young man and he saw and behold the mountain was full of horses and chariots of fire all around Elisha.

I Chronicles 16:10 - Let the hearts of those rejoice who seek the LORD! Seek the LORD and His strength seek His face evermore. Remember His marvelous works which He has done

I Chronicles 16:25 - For the LORD is great and greatly to be praised; He is also to be feared above all gods...but the LORD made the heavens Honor and majesty are before Him. STRENGTH and GLADNESS are in His place

I Chronicles 28:7-9 - Moreover I will establish his kingdom forever, if he is steadfast to observe my commandments and my judgments as it is this day. Be careful to seek out all the commandments of the LORD your God that you may possess the good land and leave it as an inheritance for your children after you forever. As for you my son Silver know the God of your father and serve Him with a loyal heart and with a willing mind for the LORD searches all hearts and understands all the intent of the thoughts. If you seek Him He will be found by you...

I Chronicles 29:11 - Yours O LORD is the greatness the power and the glory the victory and the majesty, for all that is in heaven and in earth is yours. Both riches and honor come from you in your hand in power and might in your hand it is to make great and to give strength to all...for all things come from You and of Your own we have given You

II Chronicles 7:14 - If my people who are called by my name will humble themselves and pray and seek my face and turn from their wicked ways then I will hear from heaven and will forgive their sin and heal their land

II Chronicles 16:9 - For the eyes of the LORD run to and fro throughout the whole earth to show Himself strong on behalf of those whose heart is loyal to Him

II Chronicles 20:12 - Oh our God will you not judge them for we have no power against this great multitude that is coming against us nor do we know what to do but our eyes are upon you

II Chronicles 20:15 - Thus says the LORD to you, do not be afraid or dismayed because of this great multitude for the battle is not yours but God's...tomorrow go down against them...you will not need to fight in this battle. Position yourselves, stand still and see the salvation of the LORD, who is with you...Believe in the LORD your God and you shall be established believe his prophets and you shall prosper

Nehemiah 13:2 - However our God turned the curse into a blessing

Job 26:7 - He hangs the earth on nothing. By His spirit He adorned the heavens; indeed these are the mere edges of His ways, and how small a whisper we hear of Him! But the thunder of His power who can understand?

Job 29:3 - By His light I walked through darkness. Just as I was in the days of my prime when the friendly counsel of God was over my tent.

Job 29:5 - When the almighty was yet with me, when my children were around me. When my steps were bathed with croam and the rock poured out the rivers of oil for me!

Psalm 1 - Blessed is the man who walks not in the counsel of the ungodly, nor stand in the path of sinners, nor sits in the seat of the scornful. But his delight is in the law of the LORD and in His law he meditates day and night. He shall be like a tree planted by rivers of water that brings forth its fruit in its season, whose leaf also shall not wither and whasotever he does shall prosper.

Psalm 2:3 - But you oh LORD are a shield for me

Psalm 4:3 - But know that the LORD has set apart for Himself him who is godly. The LORD will hear when I call to Him.

Psalm 4:6 - LORD lift up the light of your countenance upon us. You have put gladness in my heart.

Psalm 4:7 - I will both lie down in peace and sleep; for you alone oh LORD make me dwell in safety

Psalm 5:11 - Let those also who love your name be joyful in you. For you oh LORD will bless the righteous; with favor you shall surround him as with a shield.

Psalm 11:7 - For the LORD is righteous, He loves righteousness; His countenance beholds the upright

Psalm 16:3 - As for the saints who are on the earth, they are the excellent ones in whom is all my delight

Psalm 18:2 - The Lord is my Rock and my fortress and my deliverer. My God, my strength in whom I will trust. My shield and the horn of my salvation my stronghold

Psalm 18:6 - In my distress I called upon the LORD and cried out to my God...The LORD thundered from heaven and the Most High uttered His voice hailstones and coals of fire He sent out His arrows and scattered his foe, lighting in abundance and He vanquished them. He drew me out of many waters. He delivered me from my strong enemy for they were too strong for me. But the LORD was my support. He delivered me because He delighted in me.

Psalm 27:14 - Wait on the LORD; be of good courage and He shall strengthen your heart; wait, I say on the LORD!

Psalm 28:7 - The LORD is my strength and my shield; my heart trusted in Him and I am helped; therefore my heart greatly rejoices and with my song I will praise Him. The LORD is their strength and He is the saving refuge of His anointed.

Psalm 30:5 - His favor is for life now in my prosperity I said I shall never be moved LORD by your favor you have made my mountain stand strong

Psalm 30:11 - You have turned for me my mourning into dancing

Psalm 32:11 - Be glad in the LORD and rejoice your righteousness; and shout for joy all you upright in heart!

Psalm 33:1 - Rejoice in the LORD O you righteous! For praise from the upright is beautiful.

Psalm 34:7 - The angel of the LORD encamps all around those who fear Him and delivers them...there is no want to those who fear Him...

Psalm 35:27 - Let them say continually let the LORD be magnified who has pleasure in the prosperity of His servants...

Psalm 36:6 - your righteousness is like the great mountains; your judgements are a great deep. The children of men put their trust under the shadow of your wings for with you is the fountain of life. In your light we see light. Oh continue your loving kindnesses to those who know you and your righteousness to the upright in heart

Psalm 37:23 - The steps of a good man are ordered by the LORD and He delights in his way. Though he falls he shall not be utterly cast down. For the LORD upholds him with His hand

Psalm 37:34 - Wait on the LORD and keep His way and He shall exalt you

Psalm 37:37 - Mark the blameless man and observe the upright; for the future of that man is peace

Psalm 44:3 - For they did not gain possession of the land by their own sword...but it was your right hand, your arm and the light of your countenance because you favored them

Psalm 45:7 - You love righteousness and hate wickedness; therefore God, your God has anointed you with the oil gladness more than your companions

Psalm 46:1 - God is our refuge and strength a very present help in trouble. Therefore we will not fear, even though the earth be removed

Psalm 46:10 - Be still and know that I am God; I will be exalted among that nations, I will be exalted in the earth! The LORD of hosts with us; the God of Jacob is our refuge

Psalm 48:1 - Great is the LORD and greatly to be praised

Psalm 48:14 - For this is God, our God Forever and ever. He will be our guide even to death

Psalm 51:10 - Create in me a clean heart o God and renew a steadfast spirit within me

Psalm 56:9 - When I cry out to you, then my enemies will turn back; this I know because God is for me

Psalm 57:1 - Be merciful to me, o God be merciful to me! For my soul trusts in you; and in the shadow of your wings I will make my refuge until these calamities have passed by

Psalm 64:10 - The righteous shall be glad in the LORD and trust in Him and all the upright in heart shall glory

Psalm 65:4, 5, 7 - Blessed is the man you choose and cause to approach you that he may dwell in your courts. By awesome deeds in righteousness you will answer us O God of our salvation. Being clothed with power you who stills the noise of the seas

Psalm 68:13 - Though you lie down among the sheepfolds, you will be like the wings of a dove covered with silver, her feathers with yellow gold

Psalm 71:19 - Also your righteousness o God is very high you who have done great things o God who is like you?

Psalm 72:18 - Blessed be the LORD God...who only does wondrous things!

Psalm 73:16-17 - When I thought how to understand this it was too painful for me – until I went into the sanctuary of God. Then I understood...

Psalm 75:6-7 -For exaltation comes neither from the east nor from the west nor from the south. But GOD is the judge: he puts down one, and exalts another

Psalm 77:13 - Who is so great a God as our God? You are the God who does wonders

Psalm 78:52 - But He made His own people go fourth like sheep, and guided them in the wilderness like a flock... then the LORD awoke as from sleep like a mighty man who shouts because of wine and He beat back His enemies; He put them to a perpetual reproach

Psalm 84:2 - My soul longs yes even faints for the courts of the LORD; my heart and my flesh cry out for the living God

Psalm 84:11-12 - For the LORD God is a sun and shield; the LORD will give grace and glory; NO GOOD THING WILL HE WITHHOLD FROM THOSE WHO WALK UPRIGHTLY. Oh LORD of hosts, blessed is the man who trusts in you!

Psalm 89:5-10 - And the heavens will praise your wonders o LORD...for who in the heavens can be compared to the LORD? Who among the sons of the mighty can be likened to the LORD? God is greatly to be feared in the assembly of the saints and to be held in reverence by all those around Him. O LORD God of hosts who is mighty like you, O LORD? Your faithfulness also surrounds you. You rule the raging of the sea; when its waves rise, you still them

Psalm 89:15 - Blessed are the people who know the joyful sound! They walk O LORD in the light of your countenance. In your name they rejoice all day long. And in your righteousness they are exalted. For you are the glory of their strength and in your favor our horn is exalted. For our shield belongs to the the LORD and Our King to the Holy one of Israel.

Psalm 91:1 - He who dwells in the secret place of the most High shall abide under the shadow of the Almighty. I will say of the LORD He is my refuge and my fortress; my God in Him I will trust. Surely He shall deliver you...He shall cover you with His feathers and under His wings you shall take refuge. His truth shall be your shield and buckles

Psalm 91:5 - You shall not be afraid of the terror by night, nor the arrow that flies by day...

Psalm 91:4 - His truth shall be your shield and buckler

Psalm 91:14 - Because he has set his love upon me, therefore I will deliver him. I will set him on high because he has known my name. He shall call upon me and I will answer him. I will be with him in trouble; I will deliver him and honor him with long life I will satisfy him

Psalm 92:13 - Those who are planted in the house of the LORD shall flourish in the courts of our God. They shall still bear fruit in old age

Psalm 96:6 - Honor and majesty are before Him strength and beauty are in His sanctuary

Psalm 98:4 - Shout joyfully to the LORD all the earth break fourth in song, rejoice and sing praises

Psalm 100:4 - Enter His gates with thanks and into His courts with praise, Be thankful to Him and bless His name for the LORD is good His mercy is everlasting...

Psalm 103:2 - Bless the LORD O my soul and forget not all His benefits who forgives all your iniquities who heals all your diseases who redeems your life from destruction who crowns you with loving kindness

Psalm 105:13-15 - When they went from one nation to another from one kingdom to another people He permitted no one to do them wrong: Yes, He rebuked kings for their sakes, saying "Do not touch my anointed ones and do my prophets no harm"

Psalm 106:4 - Remember me O LORD with the favor you have toward your people...that I may see the benefit of your chosen ones that I may rejoice in the greatness of your nation that I may glory with your inheritance

Psalm 107:6 - Then they cried out to the LORD in their trouble and He delivered them out of their distress and He led them forth by the right way

Psalm 107:9 - For He satisfies the longing soul and fills the hungry soul with goodness

Psalm 108:12 - Give us help from trouble for the help of man is useless, through God we do valiantly for it is He who shall tread down our enemies

Psalm 112:1 - Blessed is the man who fears the LORD, who delights greatly in His commandments

Psalm 112:2 - The generation of the upright will be blessed wealth and riches will be in his house

Psalm 113:5-6 - Who is like the LORD our God who dwells on high who humbles himself to behold the things that are in the heavens and in the earth

Psalm 121:2 - My help comes from the Lord who made heaven and earth. He will not allow your foot to be moved; He who keeps you will not slumber

Psalm 138:3 - In the day when I cried out, You answered me, and made me bold with strength in my soul.

Psalm 145:2-3 - Every day I will bless You, and I will praise Your name forever and ever. Great is the Lord and greatly to be praised; and His greatness is unsearchable

Psalm 145:6 - Men shall speak of the might of Your awesome acts and I will declare Your greatness

Proverbs 2:7 – The Lord is a shield to those who walk uprightly

Proverbs 3:5-6 - Trust in the Lord with all your heart and do not lean on your own understanding; in all your ways, acknowledge Him and he will make your path straight

Proverbs 3:26 - For the Lord will be your confidence

Proverbs 8:17 - I love those who love Me, and those who seek Me diligently will find Me. Riches and honor are with Me, enduring riches and righteousness. My fruit is better than gold... And my revenue than choice silver

Proverbs 8:20 - I traverses (travel along) the way of righteousness in the midst of the paths of justice that I may cause those who love me to inherit wealth; that I may fill their treasuries

Proverbs 22:4 - By humility and the fear of the Lord are riches and honor and life

Isaiah 40:28-29 - Have you not known? Have you not heard? The everlasting God, the Lord the Creator of the ends of the earth neither faints nor is weary. His understanding is unsearchable. He gives power to the weak and to those who have no might, He increases strength

Isaiah 41:8-10 - But you are my servant whom I have chosen. I have chosen you and have not cast you away. Do not fear for I am with you. Do not anxiously look about for

I am your God. I will strengthen you, surely, I will help you. Surely, I will uphold you with My righteous right hand

Isaiah 41:11 - Behold all these who were incensed against You shall be ashamed and disgraced; they shall be as nothing, and those who strive with You shall perish. You shall sook them and not find them. Those who contend with you, those who war against you shall be as nothing
For I the Lord your God will hold your right hand saying, "fear not I will help you... You shall rejoice in the Lord and glory in the Holy One of Israel

Isaiah 42:6 - I the Lord have called you in righteousness, and will hold your hand; I will keep you and give you as a covenant to the people. As a light to the Gentiles, to open blind eyes to bring out prisoners from the prison. Those who sit in darkness from the prison house. I am the Lord, that is My name; and My glory I will not give to another

Isaiah 43:1 - But now thus says the Lord who created you and He who formed you, fear not for I have redeemed you, I have called you by your name. You are mine. When you pass through the waters, I will be with you.

Isaiah 43:2 - Whenever you pass through the waters, I will be with you, and through the rivers, they shall not overflow you. When you walk through the fire, you shall not be burned nor shall the flame scorch you. FOR I AM THE LORD YOUR GOD, THE HOLY ONE OF ISRAEL, YOUR SAVIOR.

Isaiah 43:10-13 - "You are My witness," says the Lord, "And My Servant whom I have chosen, that you may know and believe Me and understand that I am He. Before Me there was no God formed. Nor shall there be after me. I, even I am He. I am the Lord and besides Me there is no other Savior...

Isaiah 44:2 - Thus says the Lord who made you and formed you from the womb, who helped you: FEAR NOT Silver, the one whom I have chosen. For I will pour water on him who is thirsty, and floods on the dry ground. I will pour My Spirit upon your descendants and My blessings on your offspring; they will spring up amongst the grass like willows by the watercourse.

Isaiah 44:8 - Do not fear nor be afraid; have I not told you from that time and declared it? You are My witnesses. Is there a God besides Me? Indeed, there is no other rock. I know not one.

Isaiah 45:1-3 - Thus says the Lord to His anointed whose right hand I have held – to subdue nations before him and lose the armor of kings, to open before him the double doors, so that the gates will not be shut; I will go before you and make the crooked places straight. I will break in pieces the gates of bronze and cut the bars of iron asunder I will give you the treasure of darkness and hidden riches of secret places, that you may know that I am the Lord, who called you by your name. I am the God of Israel

Isaiah 45:4 - I have called you by your name; I have named you though you have not known Me. I am the Lord and there is no other. There is no God besides Me. I will gird you, though you have not known Me That they may know from the rising of the sun to its setting that there is none besides Me. I am the Lord and there is no other I form the light and create the darkness. I make peace and create calamity

Isaiah 46:9-11 - For I am God and there is no other; I am God and there is none like Me, declaring the end from the beginning and from the ancient times, things that are not yet done. Indeed I have spoken it; I will also bring it to pass, I have purposed it, I will also do it

Isaiah 48:17 - Thus says the Lord your Redeemer, the Holy One of Israel: I am the Lord your God, Who teaches you to profit, who leads you by the way you should go.

Oh, that you had heeded My commandments! Then your peace would have been like a river and your righteousness like the waves of the sea...

Isaiah 49:15 - Can a woman forget her nursing child, and not have compassion on the son of her womb? Surely, they may forget Yet I will not forget you. See, I have inscribed you on the palms of My hands...

Isaiah 49:26 - For I will contend with him who contends with you... All flesh shall know that I the Lord am your Savior and your Redeemer, the Mighty One...

Isaiah 51:1 - Listen to Me you who follow righteousness, you who seek the Lord, look to the Rock from which you were hewn

Isaiah 51:12 - I, even I am He who comforts you. Who are you that you should be afraid?

Isaiah 52:12 - For the Lord will go before you and the God of Israel will be your rear guard

Isaiah 54:10 - "For the mountains shall depart and the hills be removed but My kindness shall not depart from you nor shall My covenant of peace be removed," says the Lord who has mercy on you

Isaiah 54:17 - No weapon formed against you shall prosper... And every tongue which rises against you in judgment you shall condemn. This is the heritage of the servants of the Lord and their righteousness is from Me

Isaiah 55:12 - For you shall go out with JOY and be led out with peace. The mountains and hills shall break forth into singing before you, and all the trees of the field shall clap their hands...

Isaiah 57:15 - For thus says the High and Lofty One who

inhabits eternity, whose name is Holy, I dwell in the high
and holy place with him who has a contrite and humble
spirit

Isaiah 58:8 - Then your light shall break forth like the
morning, your healing shall spring forth speedily and your
righteousness shall go before you. The glory of the Lord
shall be your rear guard. Then you shall call and the Lord
will answer; you shall cry and He will say, "Here I am"

Isaiah 59:16 - He saw that there was no man and wondered
that there was no intercessor. Therefore, His own right
arm brought salvation for Him and His own righteousness
sustained Him. For He put on righteousness as a
breastplate, and a helmet of salvation on His head; He put
on garments of vengeance for clothing and was clad with
zeal as a cloak...

Isaiah 60:1 - Arise, shine; for your light has come! And
the glory of the Lord is risen upon you. For behold, the
darkness shall cover the earth and deep darkness the
people; but the Lord will arise over you and His glory will
be seen upon you

Isaiah 60:15 - Whereas you have been forsaken and hated,
so that no one went through you, I will make you an eternal
excellence, a joy for many generations you shall know that I
the Lord and your Savior and your Redeemer the Might One
of Jacob

Isaiah 61:1 - The Spirit of the Lord God is upon Me because
the Lord has anointed Me to preach good tiding to the poor;
He has sent Me to heal the brokenhearted, to proclaim
liberty to the captives, and the opening of the prison to
those who are bound; to proclaim the acceptable year of the
Lord, and the day of vengeance of our God, to comfort all
who mourn

Isaiah 64:4 - For since the beginning of the world, men have not heard nor perceived by the ear, nor has the eye seen any God besides You, who acts for the one who waits for Him. You meet him who rejoices and does righteousness, who remembers you in your ways

Isaiah 64:7   And there is no one who calls on your name who stirs himself up to take hold of you

Jeremiah 5:14 - Therefore, thus says the Lord God of Hosts, "Because you speak this word, behold, I will make My words in your mouth fire and this people wood."

Jeremiah 15:16 - Your word was to me the joy and rejoicing of my heart. For I am called by Your name, O Lord God of Hosts

Jeremiah 16:19 - O Lord my strength and my fortress, my refuge in the day of affliction

Jeremiah 20:11-12 - But the Lord is with me, as a mighty awesome One; but O Lord of Hosts, You who test the righteous and see the mind and heart

Jeremiah 23:28-29 - "What is the chaff to the wheat?" says the Lord. "Is not my Word like a fire?" says the Lord. "And like a hammer that shatters rock?"

Jeremiah 30:16-17 - All who prey upon you, I will make prey. For I will restore health to you, and heal you

Jeremiah 31:3 - The Lord has appeared of old to me saying, "Yet, I have loved you with an everlasting love. Therefore, with lovingkindness I have drawn you, again I will build you and you shall be rebuilt."

Jeremiah 32:17 - Ah, Lord God! Behold, You have made the heavens and the earth by Your great power and outstretched arm. There is nothing too hard for you

Jeremiah 33:3 - Call to Me and I will answer you and show you great and mighty things...

Daniel 10:19-20 - And he (the angel) said, "Oh man greatly beloved, fear not, peace be with you, be strong; yes, be strong!" So when he spoke to me, I was strengthened and said, "Let my lord speak for you have strengthened me"

Daniel 11:32 - But the people who know their God shall be strong and carry out great exploits

Hosea 11:9 - For I am God, not man, the Holy One in your midst

Joel 2:25 - So I will restore to you the years that the swarming locust has eaten... You shall eat in plenty and be satisfied and praised the name of the Lord your god who has dealt wondrously with you ...I am the Lord your God and there is no other

Micah 7:8 - Do not rejoice over me my enemy; when I fall I will arise; when I sit in darkness, the Lord will be a light to me

Habakkuk 1:5 - Look among the nations and watch – be utterly astounded! For I will work a work in your days which you would not believer though it were told to you

Zechariah 2:5 - For I, says the Lord, I will be a wall of fire all around her, and I will be the glory in her midst
Zechariah 2:8 - For thus says the Lord of Hosts. He sent me after glory to the nations which plunder you, for he who touches you touches the apple of His eye

Malachi 1:11 - For from the rising of the sun even to its going down, My name shall be great... In every place, incense shall be offered to My name and a pure offering for My name shall be great...

Malachi 2:5-6 - My covenant was with him, one of life and peace, and I gave them to him that he might fear me. So he feared Me and was reverent before My name. The law of truth was in his mouth, and injustice was not found on his lips. He walked with Me in peace an equity and turned many away from iniquity

Matthew 5:16 - Let your light shine in such a way that they may see your good works and glorify your Father who is in heaven

Matthew 8:10 - When Jesus heard it, HE MARVELED and said to those who followed, "Assuredly I say to you, I have not found such great faith, not even in Israel!"

Matthew 8:26 - Jesus said to them, "Why are you fearful O you of little faith?" Then Jesus arose and rebuked the winds and the sea and there was a GREAT CALM

Matthew 9:22 - And when Jesus saw her, He said, "Be of good cheer daughter. Your faith has made you well." And the woman was made well from that hour

Matthew 9:29 - And Jesus said to them, "Do you believe that I am able to do this?" They said to Him, "Yes Lord." Then He touched their eyes saying, "According to your faith, let it be to you." And their eyes were opened

Matthew 11:28-29 - Come to Me all you who are weary and heavy laden and I will give you rest. Take My yoke upon you and learn from Me, for I am gentle and humble of spirit, and you shall find rest for your souls

Matthew 14:35 - And when men of that place recognized Him, they sent out into all the surrounding region, brought to Him all who were sick, and begged Him that they might only touch the hem of His garment. And as many as touched it, WERE MADE PERFECTLY WELL

Matthew 15:28 - Then Jesus answered and said to her, "O woman, great is your faith! Let it be to you as you desire." And her daughter was healed from that very hour

Matthew 23:11-12 - But he who is greatest amongst you shall be your servant. And whoever exalts himself, will be humbled and he who humbles himself will be exalted

Matthew 28:5-6 - But the angel answered and said to the women, "Do not be afraid, for I know that you seek Jesus who was crucified" He is not here, for He has risen

Mark 12:29-30 - O Israel, the Lord Our God, the Lord is One. And you shall love the Lord your God with all your heart, with all your soul, with all your mind, and with all your strength...

Luke 6:12 - Now it came to pass in those days that He went out to the mountain to pray and continued all night in payer to God

Luke 6:19 - And the whole multitude sought to touch Him for power went out from Him and healed them all

Luke 17:5 - And the Apostles said to the Lord, "Increase our faith." So the Lord said, "If you have faith as a mustard seed, you can say to this mulberry tree, 'Be pulled up by the roots and be planted in the sea,' and it would obey you"

Luke 18:42 - Jesus said, "Receive your sight. Your faith has made you well." And immediately he received his sight...

John 4:23-24 - But the hour is coming and now is, when the true worshipers will worship the Father in spirit and truth; for the Father is seeking such to worship Him. God is Spirit, and those who worship Him must worship in Spirit and truth

John 8:29 - I always do those things that please the Father

John 10:10 - I came that they may have life and that they may have it more abundantly

John 14:6 - Jesus said to him, "I am the way, the truth and the life. No one comes to the Father expect through ME"

John 14:16 - And I will pray to the Father and He will give you another Comforter that He may abide with you forever

John 15:11 - These things I have spoken to you that My joy may remain in you and that your joy may be full

Acts 3:19 - Repent therefore and be converted that your sins may be blotted out, so that times of refreshing may come from the presence of the Lord

Acts 4:33 - And with great power, the apostles gave witness to the resurrection of the Lord Jesus and great grace was upon them all

Romans 4:17 - God, who gives life to the dead and calls those things that do not exist as though they did

Romans 4:20-21 - Yet with respect to the promise of God, he did not waiver in unbelief, but grew strong in faith, giving glory to God and being fully assured that what God had promised, He was able also to perform

Romans 5:3 - We also glory in tribulations, knowing that tribulation produces perseverance; and perseverance, character, and character hope...

Romans 8:28 - And we know that all things work together for good to those who love God, to those who are called according to His purpose

Romans 8:31 - If God is for us, who can be against us

Romans 8:32 - He who did not spare His own Son but delivered Him up for us all, how will He not also with Him, freely give us all things

Romans 8:37 - We are more than conquerors through Him who loves us

Romans 8:38-39 - For I am convinced that neither death, nor life, nor angels, nor principalities, nor powers, nor things present, nor things to come, nor height, nor depth, nor any other created thing, shall be able to separate us from the love of God, which is in Christ Jesus our Lord

Romans 10:9-10 - If you confess with your mouth the Lord Jesus and believe in your heart that God has raised Him from the dead, you will be saved

I Corinthians 2:4 - And my speech and my words are not of persuasive preaching of human wisdom, but in demonstration of the Spirit and of power, that your faith should not be in the wisdom of men, but in the power of God

I Corinthians 16:13 - Watch, stand fast in the faith, be brave, be strong, let all you do be done with love

II Corinthians 5:7 - For we walk by faith, not by sight

Ephesians 1:7 - In Him we have redemption through His blood, the forgiveness of sins, according to the riches of His grace

Ephesians 2:10 - For we are His workmanship, created in Christ Jesus for good works which God prepared beforehand that we should walk in them

Ephesians 6:13 - Therefore, take up the whole armor of God, that you may be able to withstand the evil day and having done all to stand. Stand therefore, having girded your waist with truth, having put on the breastplate of righteousness, and having shod your feet with the preparation of the Gospel of peace. Above all, taking the shield of faith with which, you will be able to quench all fiery darts of the wicked one. And take the helmet of salvation and the sword of the Spirit, which is the Word of God, praying always with all prayer and supplication in the Spirit, being watchful to this end with all perseverance and supplication for all the saints

Philippians 1:6 - Being confident of the this very thing that He who has begun a good work in you will compete it until the day of Jesus Christ

Philippians 3:13 - Brethren, I do not count myself to have apprehended but one thing I do, FORGETTING THOSE THINGS WHICH ARE BEHIND AND REACHING FORWARD TO THOSE THINGS WHICH ARE AHEAD, I PRESS TOWARD THE GOAL FOR THE PRIZE OF THE CALL OF GOD IN CHRIST JESUS

Philippians 4:1 - Therefore, my beloved and longed for brethren, my JOY AND CROWN SO STAND FIRM IN THE LORD my beloved

Philippians 4:11 - ...I have learned in whatever state I am to be content

Philippians 4:13 - I can do all things through Christ who strengthens me

Colossians 1:10 - Walk worthy of the Lord, fully pleasing Him, being fruitful in every good work and increasing in the knowledge of God; strengthened with all might according to His glorious power for all patience and longsuffering with joy

II Thessalonians 3:3 - But the Lord is faithful, who will establish you and guard you from the evil one

II Timothy 4:7 - I have fought the good fight. I have finished the race. I have kept the faith. Finally, there is laid up for me the crown of righteousness, which the Lord, the righteous Judge will give to me on that day, and not to me only, but also to all who have loved His appearing

II Timothy 4:17 – But the Lord stood with me and strengthened me so that the message might be preached fully through me. Also, I was delivered out of the mouth of the lion and the Lord will deliver me from every evil work and preserve me for His heavenly kingdom

Hebrews 1:9 - You have loved righteousness and hated lawlessness, therefore, God Your God, has anointed You with the oil of gladness more than Your companions

I Peter 1:5-9 - In this you greatly rejoice though now for a little while, if need be you have been grieved by various trials, that the genuineness of your faith, being much more precious than gold that perishes, though it is tested by fire, may be found to praise, honor, glory at the revelation of Jesus Christ

I Peter 2:9 - But you are a chosen generation a royal priesthood, a holy nation, His own special people that you may proclaim the praises of Him who called you out of darkness into His marvelous light

I John 1:5 - This is the message which we have heard from Him and declare to you that, GOD IS LIGHT, and in Him, IS NO DARKNESS AT ALL

Revelation 1:8 - "I am the Alpha and the Omega, the Beginning and the End," says the Lord, "Who is and who was, and who is to come, the Almighty"

Revelation 2:18-19 - These things says the Son of God who has eyes like a flame of fire and His feet like fine brass.

Revelation 3:12 - He who overcomes, I will make him a pillar in the temple of My God

Revelation 10:1 - I saw still another mighty angel coming down from heaven, clothed with a cloud and a rainbow was on his head, his face was like the sun and his feet like pillars of fire

Revelation 21:5-7 - Then He who sat on the throne said, "Behold, I make all things new." And He said to me, "Write, for these things are true and faithful." And he said to me, "It is done! I am the Alpha and Omega, the BEGINNING AND END. I will give of the fountain of the water of life freely to him who thirsts. He who overcomes shall inherit all things, and I will be his God and he shall be My son"

Revelation 22:16-17 - I JESUS HAVE SENT MY ANGEL TO TESTIFY TO YOU THESE THINGS IN THE CHURCHES I AM THE ROOT AND OFFSPRING OF DAVID, THE BRIGHT AND MORNING STAR

Acknowledgements

~~~

I am so thankful for my kids whom I love deeply. Their names are, Silver, Calvary, and Makenzie. After God, they are the love of my life; everything I do has them in mind. When I set out to write this book, my goal was to show them, in some small way, that anything is possible. Now that it is complete, I have them to thank as I may not have attempted this labor of love without them. I am also so thankful for my former wife who has forgiven me and blessed me in so many amazing ways. She is truly an amazing woman. Also, a host of Christians in my life that helped me grow spiritually. Their influence upon my life has been nothing short of magnificent.

Thank you Pastor Dea Warford for teaching me to pray for an hour a day. Also Pastor Colin Campbell for teaching me to memorize a hundred scriptures. To Brandi Runner, I am grateful for helping me turn this book from something resembling a computer-like manuscript, into a tremendous flow of my life experiences. Last but not least, I'd like to thank my mom, whom I love so very much for her protection and guidance during some of the toughest times of my life.

Silver A. Fisher

For further information contact Silver at:
www.SilverFisher.com